The Foreign Trade of Communist China

ITS IMPACT ON THE FREE WORLD

PRAEGER SPECIAL STUDIES IN
INTERNATIONAL ECONOMICS

The Foreign Trade
of Communist China

ITS IMPACT ON
THE FREE WORLD

PAULINE LEWIN
formerly of The Economist Intelligence Unit

Prepared by
THE ECONOMIST INTELLIGENCE UNIT *for*

FREDERICK A. PRAEGER, PUBLISHER
New York • London

The purpose of the Praeger Special Studies is to make specialized research monographs in international economics and politics available to the academic, business, and government communities. For further information, write to the Special Projects Division, Frederick A. Praeger, Publisher, 111 Fourth Ave., New York, N. Y. 10003.

FREDERICK A. PRAEGER, *Publisher*
111 Fourth Ave., New York 3, N. Y., U.S.A.
77-79 Charlotte Street, London W.1, England

Published in the United States of America in 1964
by Frederick A. Praeger, Inc., Publisher

Library of Congress Catalog Card Number: 64–16671

Printed in The United States of America

CONTENTS

Chapter		Page
	Statistical Appendix	95

The Foreign Trade of Communist China

ITS IMPACT ON THE FREE WORLD

TIME FOR CHANGE

The coming years promise the re-entry of China into the main-stream of international trade after a decade in which ideology above all else has determined the direction of exchanges. In 1953, the Soviet Union and Eastern Europe supplied some 80 per cent of China's imports and took two-thirds of its exports (the figures for 1938 were 8 per cent and 3 per cent, respectively); by 1961 they provided only half of all imports though they still took some 60 per cent of exports. The trend away from trading with the Communist world continued during 1962 and 1963 and a new pattern of Chinese trade appears to be emerging, in which the western world and Japan will play a much larger part. It seems pertinent to enquire what this may entail for world trade.

The present is an opportune moment to undertake such an enquiry in that Chinese industry appears to have weathered much of the disorganization and dislocation caused by the ill-judged Great Leap while agriculture, after three disastrous years in 1959, 1960 and 1961, had average, though not bountiful, harvests in 1962 and 1963. The economy is moving forward again: the speed of progress is impossible to judge; but the trend of development, with agriculture the acknowledged basis of the economy, is clearly more suited to Chinese conditions; and thus, in the absence of natural disasters, is likely to yield more solid -   though in the short term perhaps slower - results than the earlier slavish adherence to the theory that development must be based on heavy industry.

At no time has China been a major world trader, though at certain times it has contributed significant quantities of certain, mainly minor, products entering into world trade. With more than a fifth of the world's population, the country accounted, according to U.N. estimates, for some 1.9 per cent of world exports in 1959, the last year before bad harvests reduced export potential. This is better than India's 1.0 per cent, but it is less than the Soviet Union's share (4.5 per cent) and is insignificant beside the United States' proportion of 15.5 per cent or even that of the United Kingdom - 7.8 per cent - with a population one thirteenth part that of China. Total foreign trade turnover is equal to less than $7 per head of the Chinese population, while in India it reaches $8 per head, in the U.S.S.R. $55, in the United States $195, and in Britain soars to $420 per head. It may be noted in passing that if China had a per head foreign trade turnover as big as that of the U.S.S.R. its total

trade turnover would be on a par with that of the United States.
However, it will be many years before this happens and China may
never become a major trading nation like the United States, Japan,
or the industrialized countries of Western Europe whose standard of
living depends on a large volume of world trade. It may even have
the natural resources, though this is not yet established, to permit
a policy of self-sufficiency should its government so wish; but the
introduction of such a policy could only be a long-term aim. For
the foreseeable future China must trade, and because the country is
so vast, even if poor, it could become a very important factor in
world trade.

The Chinese Government has greatly modified its ideas of the
speed at which economic development can be pushed through since
the early days of the Great Leap; indeed, some of its spokesmen
seem to voice the other extreme. Foreign Minister Chen Yi
recently said that China would need some eighty years to reach the
degree of industrialization of Switzerland (surely an odd choice for
comparison, for it is impossible to envisage the Chinese economy
being developed on lines that would produce an industrial structure
in any way akin to that forced on Switzerland by geography). While
this may over-state the case as much as earlier boasts understated it, it seems reasonable to assume that the world will have
some decades in which to absorb the full impact of China's economic
growth on international trade and to adjust to the new conditions.
But in the meanwhile world markets in individual products may be
severely jolted - for a longer or a shorter period, for better or
for worse - by Chinese actions. For some products China may
show a steady demand, mounting as industrial production rises, for
example for rubber and cotton; for others it may erupt onto the
market with massive requirements. An obvious example is provided
by recent Chinese purchases of grain from Canada and Australia,
which, wholly unexpectedly, helped to dissolve the incubus of grain
surpluses that hung over the political and economic scene in the two
countries. China could in time have a decisive impact on world
coffee and cocoa markets, even if only a small proportion of the
650-odd million Chinese acquired a taste, which the government
appears to be fostering, for such un-Chinese drinks. It could
become a factor in the world petroleum market.

When a purchaser as large as China intervenes for the first time
in any market, the question must arise how long will it remain there:
is production to be geared to a new level of demand? With some
agricultural products it may reasonably be asked whether China
will turn the tables and itself make large offers on the world market,
if only sporadically when exceptionally favourable weather sends
farm output racing ahead of population increase and available storage

space. In a few years' time, world commodity agreements to which
China is not a party may seem as inadequate as those lacking U.S.
membership.

In the case of manufactured goods, too, a country which has to
build up as large an industrial base as China must could have a many-
sided impact on world markets. Apart from buying machinery and
continuing to sell in increasing quantities traditional and other products of its light industries, it might emerge as a dominant seller
of certain other goods in the short run. In no developing country is
it possible to hold a precise balance between capacity to produce and
demand: for example, most if not all countries that have set up their
own cement plants have experienced alternating phases of scarcity
and surplus, because it is impossible so to time major construction
projects that investment demand maintains cement plants constantly
at an economic level of operation. China already exports cement in
a small way to South East Asia; the problem could assume huge
proportions simply because the magnitude of China's own needs
dwarfs that of any other developing country, except possibly India.
Similarly with steel; even at its currently pathetically low level of
domestic consumption China finds itself from time to time with
temporary surpluses of certain grades of steel. The amounts
could well become sizable in relation to the needs of most underdeveloped countries and could disrupt the export trade of the
industrialized free world if they coincided with a slump in demand -
particularly as China would have no inhibitions about price cutting.

This monograph does not seek to forecast the size of China's
foreign trade in future years or the details of its composition or
direction; the data for a precise exercise of this kind are wholly
lacking, and moreover in the case of China the natural forces which
make for an erratic progress in foreign trade in most developing
countries are supplemented by the strong political element in trade
policy. It tries only to indicate ways in which trade may develop,
in respect of both direction and composition, and to suggest factors
which may influence the country's attitude and policy towards international economic relations. To do even this much is hazardous
when the Chinese have published no reliable statistics since 1957
and virtually none at all since 1960; the state of the domestic
economy must be gauged from the scrappy and often conflicting
statements that appear in published Chinese sources, supplemented
by reports from Hong Kong, by impressions gathered by visiting
businessmen and journalists, and even by travellers' tales. Never
in postwar years has China released more than the barest figures
relating to foreign trade and even these are of strictly limited use.
Thus it is necessary to go to the trade statistics of partner countries,
and while these are for the most part of an acceptable standard

of accuracy they do not provide a complete picture. Hazards abound
in making any firm statement about China's economy, particularly if
it purports to be based on statistics; but in the chapters that follow
a number of qualifications and footnotes that would find a place in a
profounder thesis have been sacrificed in the interests of easier
reading.

Fascinating as it would be to devote the greater part of the space
available to speculating about the future course of China's trade, the
basis for such an exercise is too slender. More prosaically, this
monograph concerns itself first with a bare summary of trade in the
pre-Communist era, then looks briefly at the development of the
Chinese economy in the 'fifties and early 'sixties before examining
the general development of postwar trade. Chapters 4 and 5 analyse
more closely recent trade with certain areas and countries and
examine Chinese aid. Finally, an attempt is made to establish the
lessons and pointers that the past holds for the future.

A bibliography lists the main sources consulted during the pre-
paration of the monograph; a statistical appendix contains tables
of China's trade with the world, of Russian trade with China,
particulars of Chinese aid and some figures relating to the level of
production in Chinese agriculture and industry.

CHAPTER 1   TRADE BEFORE COMMUNISM

THE DRAGON IN CHAINS

Although we are not here concerned to examine in detail China's foreign trade before the Communist Government came to power, it is useful to summarize the main, and often unusual, features of the organization, composition, and direction of trade in the years before the outbreak of the Sino-Japanese war in 1937 and in the immediate postwar years. The institutional framework has changed out of all recognition, but there are many aspects of China's trade that show a strong continuity, and some tenets of Communist China's foreign trade policy have their roots in the treatment that the country formerly suffered at the hands of foreigners. This aroused strong feelings of nationalism in many Chinese, regardless of their political convictions.

For nearly a century foreigners traded in, rather than with, China; the decadent Manchu dynasty could neither prevent contact with the outside world nor had it the vigour to absorb and adapt Western techniques to its own purposes or the courage and far-sightedness to allow its subjects to do so. Between the Treaty of Nanking in 1842 and the Treaty of S himonoseki in 1895, eighteen foreign powers extracted from the Chinese Government a range of privileges that no other sovereign power has ever conceded in modern times. The nationals of the so-called Treaty Powers enjoyed extra-territorial rights, jurisdiction was exercised by their own consuls, and they were exempt from Chinese taxation; in the Treaty Ports they lived and traded in their own concessions and settlements; import duties were kept low and neither imports nor goods bought by foreigners for export were subject to internal levies; ships of foreign flag plied in Chinese coastal and inland waters; and some services, notably the Customs and the Post Office, were administered by foreign staff. Under the Treaty of Shimonoseki, the Japanese acquired the right to set up industries in the Treaty Ports, a right which passed automatically to all other Treaty Powers, the most-favoured-nation principle having been in operation since 1843. It was during this period that Hong Kong, leased to the British under the Treaty of Nanking, grew to importance and came to occupy the special position in China's trade that it has never since lost.

Foreigners' privileges were at their most extensive in the first decade of this century; a gradual erosion began during the 1914-18 war, which coincided with the emergence in China of a regime that realized the need for the country itself to direct and control its own economic development. But since internal and external pressures prevented the establishment, for any length of time, of a stable government in the 'twenties or 'thirties, progress in reducing foreign influence to more usual proportions was slow, although by the 'thirties it had the backing of the Western powers (though not, of course, of Japan). Thus it was not until 1943 that the United States and Britain relinquished extra-territorial rights; the remaining Treaty Powers followed suit during the next four years.

Chinese merchants began quite early on to assume certain functions in connection with trade, in particular with importing:

> The actual process of importing and exporting, however, still remained firmly in the hands of the Western merchant through-out the nineteenth century and the early decades of the present century. It was not until after 1930 that the Chinese firms themselves began to undertake that business on any scale. At that time also the Chinese Government started to purchase direct from Western producers. Yet before the outbreak of the Second World War these developments were significant chiefly because of the new trend which they disclosed in China's foreign economic relations, for the great bulk of China's imports and exports still passed through Western firms.[1]

The financing of trade, too, was overwhelmingly in the hands of foreign banks which, at least until the 'thirties, also performed many other services normally provided by the domestic banking system. In 1931, foreign investment in China was estimated at $2.5 billion (measured in 1931 dollars), and of the total 15 per cent was in mercantile ventures and another 7 per cent in banking and finance; manufacturing accounted for 12 per cent, transport for 26 per cent. The United Kingdom was estimated to have held 37 per cent of the total, Japan 35 per cent and the United States and France each 6 per cent. Industrial as well as mercantile investment was heavily concentrated in the Treaty Ports; over a third of all foreign investment in 1931 was in Shanghai alone and much Chinese money was invested in areas where the foreign

---

1. G.C. Allen and Audrey G. Donnithorne, Western Enterprise in Far Eastern Economic Development, China and Japan.

presence ensured the maintenance of law and order. Thus, when the
Communists came to power vast areas of China were quite untouched
by industry.

ABORTIVE RENAISSANCE 1919-1937

At the end of the last century the composition of China's trade was
simple: in the early eighteen-eighties opium and cotton manufactures
each made up one third of imports, while 80 per cent of exports were
accounted for by tea   (46 per cent) and silk.

MAIN COMMODITIES IMPORTED

Percentages	1925	1928	1931	1936[a]
Cotton goods	16.3	14.2	7.6	1.5
Cotton yarn	4.4	1.6	0.3	0.2
Raw cotton	7.4	5.7	12.6	3.8
Cereals	6.8	5.7	10.6	4.1
Wheat flour	1.6	2.6	2.0	0.5
Sugar	9.5	8.3	6.0	2.2
Liquid fuel & kerosene	7.9	6.6	6.3	8.3
Transport material	1.9	2.3	2.3	5.6
Chemicals & dyes	5.6	7.5	8.0	10.8
Iron & steel, metals	4.7	5.4	6.2	13.2
Machinery	1.8	1.8	3.1	6.4
Total, including others	100.0	100.0	100.0	100.0

a. Excluding Manchurian imports. By 1936 Manchuria had been
established as a separate puppet state by the Japanese.

Source   Yu-kwei Cheng, Foreign Trade and Industrial Development
of China.

By the end of the 1914-18 war, the opium trade had been eliminated
and the market for imported cotton goods was shrinking as a result
of growing local production, encouraged by the wartime reduction in
foreign competition; on average in the years 1922-26 they accounted

for one fifth of the import bill, but raw cotton was being imported in significant quantities to feed the domestic industry, and machinery and equipment was being bought to an increasing extent. In the decade before the outbreak of the Sino-Japanese war, the pattern continued to alter; the table above clearly shows the effect, particularly on the import of textiles, of the restoration of tariff autonomy to China in 1929 and of the 1934 tariff revision.

MAIN COMMODITIES EXPORTED

Percentages	1925	1928	1931	1936[a]
Silk & silk goods	22.5	18.4	13.3	7.8
Tea	2.9	3.7	3.6	4.3
Beans & bean cake	15.9	20.5	21.4	1.3
Seeds & oil	7.9	5.8	8.4	18.7
Eggs & products	4.3	4.4	4.1	5.9
Hides, leather, skins	4.0	5.4	4.1	5.7
Ores & metals	2.9	2.1	1.6	7.7
Coal	2.6	2.9	3.0	1.6
Cotton & cotton goods	5.8	7.2	7.8	7.0
Total, including others	100.0	100.0	100.0	100.0

a. Excluding Manchurian exports.

Source Cheng, op.cit.

On the export side, the tea trade declined steadily in importance until by the 'twenties it was providing only 3 to 4 per cent of export earnings; silk, on the other hand, was still accounting for nearly a quarter of exports in the early 'twenties, but thereafter it fell sharply in importance. Beans and bean cake entered the picture in a small way at the turn of the century, and in the years immediately preceding the Japanese seizure of Manchuria were making up a fifth of exports. Eggs and products, vegetable oils, skins and furs were also significant exchange earners, but as a world supplier the country's importance was greater in respect of minor products: bristles, feathers, tung oil. Although it is no longer possible to analyse China's foreign trade in this way since data are lacking, it becomes abundantly clear in later chapters that, while the present pattern of imports is very dissimilar to that of prewar days, traditional goods still play a major part in exports, despite the growing importance of manufactured products.

The prewar export trade suffered badly from the absence of a government capable of imposing standards on producers, who were normally operating on a very small scale indeed, and seeing that they were maintained. A government bureau of testing and inspection was set up only in 1936 and by that time the silk trade had largely been lost to Japan. The egg and oilseed trades were hampered by the inability of Chinese merchants to supply given quantities on a regular basis to a uniform standard; supplies were inelastic and rising demand meant rising prices and adulteration.

DIRECTION OF TRADE

Percent-ages	1919		1931		1936[a]	
	Imports	Exports	Imports	Exports	Imports	Exports
Japan	36.3	30.9	20.0	27.4	16.3	14.5
U.S.A.	16.2	16.0	22.2	13.2	19.6	26.4
Hong Kong	22.6	20.8	15.3	16.3	1.9	15.1
U.K.	9.5	9.1	8.3	7.1	11.7	9.2
Germany	-	-	5.8	2.5	15.9	5.5
France	0.5	5.4	1.5	3.8	2.0	4.3
Total[b]	100.0	100.0	100.0	100.0	100.0	100.0

a. Excluding Manchuria.   b. Including others.

Source   Cheng, op.cit.

During the first world war Japan established a hold over the Chinese market for cotton textiles and by 1919 was supplying 36 per cent of the total import market. In that year, Hong Kong accounted for 23 per cent, the United States 16 per cent and the United Kingdom under 10 per cent. By 1931, the United States (22 per cent) had overtaken Japan (20 per cent), while both Hong Kong (15 per cent) and Britain (8 per cent) had lost further ground. Figures for later years are not strictly comparable since after 1932 Manchuria was no more a part of China and, in addition, imports via Hong Kong were attributed to their countries of origin. However,

since we later wish to speculate on the future direction of China's
trade, it is worth recording the major prewar partners.

Throughout the whole of its recorded trading history until the
advent of the Communist Government, with the exception of a few
years in the 1870s, China had an import surplus, which, in the 1920s
averaged not far short of $140 million a year (at then current prices),
and in the early 'thirties rose to an annual average of nearly $200
million. It was swollen by net imports of gold and silver, by divi-
dend transfers, and by payments of freight and insurance. Current
payment items normally in China's favour were foreign expenditure,
for foreign colonies in China spent far more than Chinese abroad,
and remittances, where sums sent home to China hugely exceeded
sums repatriated by foreigners living and working in China. These
items did not, however, yield a favourable current balance and the
deficit on payments was normally covered by foreign investment.
Only from 1934 to 1936, when there was a headlong flight of capital,
were net exports of gold and silver (mainly the latter) enough to give
a favourable balance. The reversal of the usual payments position
in the mid-1930s is sharply apparent in the table on the opposite
page.

AFTERMATH OF WAR 1946-1948

The period between 1937 and 1945 is one of such confusion, when
the area of free China fluctuated with the ebb and flow of war, that it
need not concern us here, and the immediate postwar years hold
comparatively little interest. For the economy as a whole, their
most important feature was the appalling inflation; it had begun with
the outbreak of war in 1937 and by mid-1945 the note issue had mul-
tiplied nearly 250 times. The postwar budgetary deficits and failure
to revive production led to a six-hundredfold increase between
December 1945 and mid-August 1948, and conditions were comparable with those in Germany in 1923; an ill-prepared currency reform
introduced by the Nationalist Government brought no relief and the
new currency unit depreciated even faster than the old. The country
was held together only with the help of foreign aid which, in the four
years after the ending of the war in the Pacific, is estimated to have
totalled $2.25 billion, of which the U.S. Government provided $2.01
billion.

In an attempt to mop up surplus purchasing power, huge quantities
of imports were brought into the country, both commercially and
under the UNRRA programme (which covered the years 1946 and 1947)
and the U.S. Commodity Aid Programme that followed it. However,

ESTIMATE OF CHINA'S INTERNATIONAL
BALANCE OF PAYMENTS

million Haikwan taels[a]; all items net	1920-23 annual average	1928	1931	1936
Trade	-242.7	-155.1	-355.2	-211.7
Gold & silver	- 49.1	-122.5	+ 90.8	+215.1
Foreign expenditure[b]	+101.9	+142.9	+134.3	+ 95.0
Remittances	+ 70.0	+166.8	+232.2	+205.4
Other[c]	- 60.1	-171.3	-122.5	- 69.2
Current balance	-180.0	-129.2	- 20.4	+234.6
Foreign loans to Chinese government	+ 40.0	+ 2.7	-	} + 38.5
New business investment	+106.7	+ 64.0	+ 28.5	
Flight of capital	-	-	-	-273.1[d]
Capital balance	+146.7	+ 66.7	+ 28.5	-234.6
Errors & omissions	+ 33.3	+ 62.5	- 8.1	d

a. Exchange rate: HKT1 = 1920: U.S. $1.24; 1923: U.S. cents 80; 1928: U.S. cents 71; 1931: U.S. cents 34; 1936: U.S. cents 46.
b. Expenditure by foreigners in China net of Chinese expenditure abroad on legations, consulates, students, tourists etc. c. Mainly servicing of foreign obligations, transfer of profits, and freight and insurance. d. Flight of capital includes transfer of government funds and may also include some errors and omissions.

Source Cheng, op. cit. adapted from Appendix II.

poor distribution facilities, and government incompetence, which made possible profiteering and hoarding, prevented imports from being used to good advantage.

VALUE OF TRADE

$ million[a]	1946	1947	1948
Imports			
Commercial	561	451	211
UNRRA	155	158	8
Commodity aid	–	–	112
Total imports	716	609	331
Exports	149	216	170

a. Exchange rates (prevailing rates weighted by monthly trade values) equivalent to: for imports, 1946 - Chinese $2,678, 1947 - Chinese $23,682, 1948 - 5.495 gold yuan per U.S.$; for exports, 1946 - Chinese $2,768, 1947 - Chinese $29,557, 1948 - 8,206 gold yuan per U.S.$.

Source Cheng, op. cit.

Exports were surprisingly large in the immediate postwar years principally because it became possible once again to move raw materials, considerable stocks of which had been immobilized in the interior in the later years of the war. These found good markets in 1946 and 1947. In addition, much of the textile industry's capacity was devoted to exports - a not particularly sensible move in the face of dire local shortages. Even so, in 1946, 1947 and 1948 exports covered only 26 per cent, 48 per cent, and 81 per cent, respectively, of commercial imports, which were slashed in 1948. At this period, the United States was overwhelmingly China's most important trading partner. On the import side, the United Kingdom, India, and South East Asia were significant suppliers of commercial goods, while Hong Kong once again became a busy centre for the trans-shipment of Chinese goods (see table over).

With seriously unbalanced trade and chaotic internal conditions, foreign exchange reserves were drawn upon to cover deficits on current payments. Holdings of gold and short-term dollar assets are reliably estimated to have plummeted from $835 million at the

DIRECTION OF TRADE

Percent-ages	1946		1947		1948	
	Imports	Exports	Imports	Exports	Imports	Exports
U.S.A.	61.4	38.7	57.0	23.3	66.5	20.1
Hong Kong	3.5	28.2	1.4	34.2	0.9	31.4
U.K.	6.5	4.4	8.5	6.5	5.5	3.9
India	7.0	5.3	6.9	3.2	6.8	3.9
S.E.Asia	3.2	4.8	5.0	10.5	5.1	20.2

Note: imports refer to total imports, including UNRRA supplies etc.; for commercial imports and data on composition of trade see Appendix 1.

Source   Cheng, op.cit.

end of 1945 to $234 million by the beginning of 1948, and they must have fallen further during the course of that year to bridge the trade gap. Before the Communist Government assumed power they had dwindled to a small sum, mainly in sterling and Hong Kong dollars, retreating Nationalists having shipped all specie and other movable assets that they could lay hands on to Taiwan.

CHAPTER **2** THE
ECONOMY
1949-1963

It will be useful before examining the development of foreign trade
since 1949 to survey briefly the progress of the economy in the fourteen years of Communist rule, or at least those aspects of it that have
a major bearing on trade. To understand why trade developed as it
did - still more to speculate on how it may evolve in future - it is
necessary to assess how far and in what respects the economy can
meet its own requirements, how far and in what respects it produces
goods surplus to its own needs. It is necessary also to look at the
part which the Government expects foreign trade to play in economic
growth and at the main economic problems that have to be faced. A
digression of this nature into the domestic economy is all the more
necessary in a country like China, where economic organization has
changed radically and where, for the past five years, statistical data
relating to the economy have been regarded as state secrets, so that
none of the normal apparatus of economic analysis is to hand.

For the sake of convenience the years to 1963 can be divided into
four periods; though a less summary treatment would certainly require
finer sub-divisions, this chapter will consider first the three years
of rehabilitation (1950 to 1952), followed by the five First Plan years
(1953 to 1957). For the latter part of this period there are statistics
that are generally agreed to be as accurate as can be expected for a
country that had no national statistical system until the State Statistical Bureau (SSB) was set up in October 1952. The third and fourth
periods, from 1958 to 1963, cover the Great Leap, the natural
calamities and retribution that followed it and the slow beginnings of
recovery. It is a time devoid of reliable statistics; the country-wide
statistical network so carefully built up by the SSB was virtually
destroyed by the decentralization that accompanied the Leap. Though
the centralists were vindicated by the fiasco of the 1958 production
statistics, and the national network has been reconstructed, strength-
ened, and expanded at the lower levels of the administrative structure, no official statistics of any general value relating to production
or foreign trade have been released since 1960; now and again a
more or less meaningless percentage creeps into an official statement
or an isolated figure of, for example, cement production may be let

fall. For the rest such figures as there are represent the estimates of students of the China scene; however carefully they may be thought out, their originators have all too little opportunity to deserve the epithet well-informed.

RECONSTRUCTION

The over-riding aim of economic policy was, and still is, to make China an industrial power within the shortest possible time, and great stress is put on self-reliance in achieving this end. The initial approach was along the Marxist-Leninist line of developing heavy industry. The first three years of the regime were concerned with three major tasks: establishing the institutional framework, stamping out hyper-inflation, and raising production to the pre-1949 peak. The economic section of the 1949 Common Programme, the organic law of the regime until it was replaced by the 1954 Constitution, laid down the framework within which the economy was to be socialized and established the priorities of outstanding problems. It set land reform in motion, as a pre-requisite of industrialization and greater production; it gave heavy industry, from mining through iron and steel, machinery and vehicles to chemicals, priority over other sectors; it instituted strict control of financial establishments, demanded a balanced budget and required the introduction of a tax policy that would finance the conclusion of the civil war, the rehabilitation of production and permit the fulfilment of the investment programme. Of foreign trade, it said that it should be controlled to protect domestic industry.

Over the period the government gained a firm hold on the economy not so much through outright nationalization as by indirect means such as tax and credit policy and the allocation of supplies and markets. It succeeded, where the Nationalists had failed hopelessly, in re-establishing a measure of confidence in the currency and the economy - and this despite the outbreak of the Korean war, which brought renewed inflationary pressure. By 1952, inflation was under control and production of some goods was at record levels, though the Communists themselves admitted failure to raise output of all major commodities to the pre-1949 peak.

These were sizable achievements but the country was hardly even on the threshold of industrialization; it had less industry than the U.S.S.R. had had in 1917 and in an area of 3.7 million square miles there were only some 15,000 miles of railway and 50,000 miles of road. Heavy industry existed only in Manchuria and the complex built up by Japan before the war had been extensively dismantled by the Russians, a factor contributing to the downfall of the

Nationalist Government; light industry was heavily concentrated in the ports, mainly Shanghai and Tientsin. Crude steel production in 1952, while then a record, was still only 1.35 million tons, coal production was 66 million tons and power output 7.3 billion kwh; statistics for the reconstruction years are not much more than estimates, but those for heavy industry are certainly among the more reliable. Cotton cloth output doubled between 1949 and 1952, but in the latter year reached less than 8 yards per head of population. In India at the time, mill production alone provided more than half as much again per head.

NATIONAL PRODUCT BY INDUSTRIAL ORIGIN 1952

Percentages	Wage Bill	Gross Domestic Product at factor cost
Agriculture, forestry, fishing	54.2	47.1
Mining & manufacturing	21.6	22.8
of which: Modern & large-scale	5.8	9.2
Construction	2.6	2.9
Transport & communications	3.3	4.7
Trade	6.5	8.3
Government services & defence	6.4	4.9
Finance, other services, etc.	5.4	9.3
Total	100.0	100.0

Source   A. Eckstein and others, The National Income of Communist China.

The overwhelmingly agricultural character of the economy at the beginning of the First Five-Year Plan is clearly shown by Alexander Eckstein's calculations of national income in 1952. At that date, 51 per cent of India's GDP was accounted for by agriculture, while in Japan the figure was 22 per cent and in the United States and Britain 5 to 6 per cent. According to Professor Eckstein's calculations, household consumption accounted for 70 per cent of China's gross national expenditure, gross fixed investment for 10 per cent.

PLANNED DEVELOPMENT

In the preamble to the First Five-Year Plan, initiated in 1953, it was envisaged that eighteen years (three Five-Year Plans plus the three years of rehabilitation) would be needed to complete the transitional period during which "step by step" were to be brought about "the socialist industrialization of the country" and "the socialist transformation of agriculture, handicrafts and capitalist industry and commerce." While it could be argued that too precipitate a leap at the second objective was at least partly responsible for slowing down progress towards the first during the late 'fifties and early 'sixties, enormous progress was made in increasing and diversifying production during the First Five-Year Plan. The plan targets were exceeded by one-fifth in industry while agriculture accomplished what was asked of it. Efforts were centred on the 694 above-norm construction projects (those in which investment exceeded a certain sum, varying from industry to industry), "the core of which are the 156 projects to be designed with the help of the Soviet Union and which will lay the preliminary groundwork for China's socialist industrialization".[1] During the five years, new heavy industries were to be established and existing plants extended; light industry was to be developed in line with growing consumer demand; all industrial capacity was to be fully used and the handicraft and small-scale sector was to be integrated in the general plan. In agriculture the cooperative movement was to be promoted and output raised; the network of transport and communications was to be improved; the socialist sector was to consolidate its leadership over the capitalist; and the stability of the market was to be maintained.

Official data expressed in 1952 prices show net material product[2] rising by an average of 8.9 per cent a year during the First Plan,

---

1. First Five-Year Plan for the Development of the National Economy of the People's Republic of China in 1953-1957.

2. National accounts as calculated by the Communists differ from normal Western practice in that they include only the net product of industry, agriculture, building and services directly involved in material production; non-material services are excluded. The figures that follow do not therefore cover the same ground as those quoted on page 16. The U.N. Commission for Asia and the Far East considers, on the analogy of India, that China's net material product in the mid-'fifties should be marked up by about one-fifth to make it comparable with net national product in the Western sense.

but growth was far from even: 1953 saw a 14 per cent rise over the
rather poor showing of 1952 (the so-called three-antis and five-antis
campaigns in that year disrupted production); the next two years
brought increases of around 6 per cent each; a spurt in 1956 yielded
another 14 per cent rise, but 1957 did not even achieve 5 per cent.
While there are reasons for supposing that the official figures lean
towards optimism, there is a fair consensus of Western academic
opinion that economic growth averaged 6 to 7 per cent annually in
real terms in the years 1952-57. This could have meant a very
sensible improvement in living standards, for population probably
did not rise by more than 2.2 per cent annually and the increase may
have been less. In fact, however, it was investment (or accumulation
in Communist terminology) that both stimulated rising growth and
benefited from it. By direct and indirect means - rationing,
taxation, the issue of compulsory loans, the creaming off of profits
of state-controlled enterprises and farms - domestic savings were
raised to unprecedented heights.

REAL NET MATERIAL PRODUCT AND INVESTMENT 1950-1957

| | Net Material Product | | Net Investment | | |
	Index 1952=100	Increase over previous year: per cent	Index 1952=100	Increase over previous year: per cent	Proportion of NMP: per cent
1950	70	18.8	26	...	2.7
1951	82	17.0	54	108	4.7
1952	100	22.0	100	86	7.2
1953	114	14.0	184	84	11.6
1954	120	5.7	208	13	12.4
1955	128	6.5	214	3	11.9
1956	146	14.0	340	59	16.6
1957	153	4.6	317	-6	14.9

... Not available.

Source SSB, Ten Great Years.

It is estimated that all but 8 per cent (representing Soviet loans)
of investment in the first eight years of Communist rule came from

domestic sources. Foreign finance may have covered 18 per cent of investment during the three years of rehabilitation, but in the First Five-Year Plan it contributed a bare 3 per cent, and repayment of the first Soviet loan began in 1954. All medium or long-term credits given by the U.S.S.R. were exhausted by the end of 1957. Funds were allocated predominantly and, as it later transpired, unwisely in favour of heavy industry with agriculture getting a pittance.

PERCENTAGE DISTRIBUTION OF INVESTMENT
1953-1957

Industry:		Building & prospecting	6
Light	7	Trade	4
Heavy	39	Culture, education,	
Transport &		health	8
communications	16	Other	12
Agriculture	8	Total	100

<u>Source</u> SSB, Ten Great Years.

The policy did, however, yield quick results. Taking 1953 as base year and working with constant price figures, the gross value of industrial output rose by 75 per cent over the succeeding four years and of agricultural output by one-fifth – what this meant in terms of physical production is seen in Appendix 2, which shows output data for some of the more important agricultural, mineral and industrial products. (Of the figures quoted in the Appendix, those relating to agriculture are the least reliable since in China, as elsewhere in the developing world, the problems of data collection in the countryside are enormous). Manufacture started of a whole range of products never before made in China, for example, steel plate for ships and car bodies, seamless alloy steel tube, water and steam turbine generators up to 15 MW, 20,000 kva transformers, numerous types of machine tool, P.V.C. etc. This growing ability to meet growing needs led to many claims to have reached a specific ratio of self-sufficiency in various products, claims which are virtually meaningless except in relation to one point in time in a country developing as fast as China.

Between 1952 and 1957, the share of state-owned enterprises in the net material product rose from under one fifth to over one third, while that of the cooperative sector made up more than 56 per cent at the end of the period against less than 2 per cent at the beginning. The capitalist sector disappeared after 1955, absorbed into the joint state-private sector, which contributed 7.6 per cent of material product in 1957. By then the individual sector, which made up 72 per cent of the total in 1952, had shrunk to under 3 per cent. It is in this last change, engineered almost wholly after the excellent 1955 harvest, that a root cause of China's recent economic crisis lies. It was part of the prelude to that extraordinary and short-lived example of national dedication to an ideal and national euphoria the Great Leap.

THE GREAT LEAP

The sweeping collectivization of agriculture in 1956, based on the theory that the more socialized a sector the greater its output must be, did not bring the expected increase in production; instead the cultivated area shrank, draught animals were slaughtered, implements were destroyed, irrigation and land reclamation were neglected and the drift to the towns gathered pace. Food production rose by only 1.3 per cent in 1957 despite less widespread weather damage than in 1956. The connection between agricultural performance and the growth of the economy as a whole forced itself increasingly on the attention of the planners; even the crude statistics available to the public suggest a strong correlation between one year's harvest and the next year's investment level.

FARM OUTPUT AND INVESTMENT

Per cent increase on previous year	1952	1953	1954	1955	1956	1957
Gross value of farm output	15.3	3.1	3.3	7.7	4.9	3.8
Investment	x	84	13	3	59	- 6

Source SSB, Ten Great Years.

The obvious remedies, either to redirect resources into agriculture or to rescind collectivization, were politically inexpedient; the government was divided within itself and contradictory policy statements were issued. The matter was resolved by an apparently spontaneous peasant movement in some parts of the country to make good some of the slackness that followed collectivization. Teams were formed to carry out land reclamation, reafforestation and irrigation

work, and manure collection; by spring planting time labour was
becoming scarce and communal restaurants, nurseries, laundries
and other services were springing up. This advance on official
thinking was seized upon by the government, which attempted to
crystallize it into a new, communistic order of rural society. In a
few months of 1958 the whole peasant community was organized
into some 26,000 rural people's communes, [3] which were concerned
not merely with agricultural matters but became all-embracing organs
of local administration, dealing as well with industry, commerce
education etc. In theory, all property was owned by the commune
and distribution was according to need, but in practice this Communist
Utopia was never achieved; it is indeed unlikely that more than a
tithe of the communes ever functioned fully. Administrative confusion and the peasant's reluctance to part with his independence were
compounded by natural disasters, and for three years the economy
lost ground. The communes, though nominally remaining the units
of rural administration, quietly disintegrated into their more manage-
able parts, the production brigade and the production team, and the
individual farmer was once again allowed to have his own small plot.

The 1958 grain harvest, thanks to clement weather, was a bumper
one. It was originally planned at 196 million tons, a modest 6 per
cent up on 1957. Sights were repeatedly raised as optimism mounted
during 1958 and progress reports exaggerated the rosiness of prospects. The first estimate of the harvest yielded the staggering total
of 375 million tons; this was confirmed in April 1959 and then slashed
in August 1959 to 250 million tons. That is the last official figure of
a Chinese harvest and few would accept it at its face value; the most
generous Western estimate is that 220 million tons of grain may have
been harvested but that considerably less reached the barns, since
unusual plenty and the spirit of the times led to unaccustomed care-
lessness in harvesting.

This inflation of progress spread through all sectors of the economy
with devastating consequences for orderly and efficient planning; the
authorities were fooled as much as anyone else. And even when output began to fall, claims continued to rise and commitments were
entered into that could not possibly be fulfilled. In the effort to
maximize output, resources of men and materials were grossly
misused (as in the backyard steel furnaces, a phenomenon of late

---

3. It is interesting to note that in an article contributed to Cuba
Socialista in 1963, the Minister of Agriculture, Liao Lu-yen, stated
that more than 70,000 people's communes were formed in 1958 - a
figure never used in earlier releases on the subject but more
plausible in view of the number of households involved.

1958 and early 1959); quality of output was disregarded and, extremely
serious for the years immediately following, maintenance and repairs
were neglected. As a crowning blow in mid-1960, the Russians withdrew technicians, blue-prints and know-how, having completed only
about half the projects planned under various agreements.

OUTPUT OF SELECTED PRODUCTS, 1957-1959

Product	Unit		1957	1958	1959
Pig iron	million tons		5.94	13.69	...
Factory	"	"	...	9.53	20.50
Indigenous	"	"	...	4.16	...
Steel	"	"	...	11.08	...
Factory	"	"	5.35	8.00	13.35
Indigenous	"	"	...	3.08	...
Coal	"	"	130.73	270.00	347.80
Factory	"	"	123.23	218.00	...
Indigenous	"	"	7.50	51.00	...
Cement	"	"	6.86	9.30	12.27
Electricity	billion kwh		19.34	27.53	41.50
Lumber	million m3		27.87	35.00	41.20
Cotton cloth	billion metres		5.05	5.70	7.50

... Not available.

Source Choh-ming Li, The Statistical System of Communist China.

PICKING UP THE PIECES

1959 saw the first of the bad harvests; and though output of some
manufactured goods continued to rise in 1960, the industrial position
began to deteriorate in that year as supplies of agricultural raw
materials became scarcer. The extent of the fall in production is
a matter of guesswork; the grain harvest may have shrunk to as
little as 155 million tons in 1960, when heavy purchases of wheat
from abroad began, before recovering to somewhere near the 1957
level in both 1962 and 1963, by which time the population had grown
by at least 60 million. The cotton harvest appears to have been
smallest in 1961 when it was perhaps less than 1.5 million tons; but

it certainly seems to have recovered sharply by 1963. Steel output is claimed to have topped 18 million tons in 1960; but this figure may include double-counting and it is quite certain that the quality of output was such that a significant proportion of it must have been unusable. The decline started in 1961 and some estimates put 1962 output at a mere 7 million to 8 million tons, though others would concede 10 million. 1963 would appear to have brought an improvement.

During the worst of the crisis, capacity was seriously underused in all branches of industry for one reason or another: in the heavy industries because of failure to maintain and repair plant during the Great Leap, lack of spares, shortage of skilled labour, the poor quality of raw material supplies, transport bottlenecks; in the light industries mainly because agriculture could not supply raw materials, domestic supplies of man-made raw materials were inadequate, and there was no foreign exchange for imports. Throughout the country, industrial plant under construction was abandoned in various stages of completion. In 1961 the situation was so precarious (the food shortage was probably at its worst that spring) that the National People's Congress did not meet at all, and in 1962 and 1963 it met only in secret. The Great Leap and the Second Five-Year Plan began to be referred to in obituary terms; and of the latter it was said that fourteen out of seventeen main targets for industrial production had been fulfilled or overfulfilled in 1959 and 1960, but that grave natural calamities in 1959, 1960 and 1961 had reduced agricultural output.

The government's remedy lay in a bold and realistic reassessment of priorities in a bid "to consolidate the gains" made in the first two years of the abortive Second Five-Year Plan. The ten-point programme for 1962 set out in detail official thinking on economic matters. Although released as a plan of action for the coming year, it summarized policies that had already been put into effect. The final point left no doubt of the shift in emphasis: "to improve the work of planning further and ensure an all-round balance between sectors of the national economy in the order of: agriculture, light industry, heavy industry." No bones are made about this complete reversal of earlier priorities; Mao himself has pointed to the indisputable fact that the present policy "conforms with the actual situation in China", and Po I-po, Vice-Premier and Chairman of the State Economic Commission, writing for the Cuban press in 1963, said that "while serving all branches of the economy, industry must concentrate mainly on serving agriculture." The other major shift, away from investment in favour of consumption, has been as explicitly expounded in the press and in speeches.

The other points in the 1962 programme laid down that agriculture's primary task was to produce more grain (to save imports), cotton (to supply light industry) and oil-bearing crops (to provide greater exports). Light industry was to make enough goods in daily use to induce the farmer to work harder. Investment of material and equipment was to be concentrated in the sectors where it was most urgently needed; labour which had migrated to the towns was to return to the agricultural front; the people were "to work energetically to fulfil the tasks in foreign trade".

Tasks for 1963 and 1964 have remained basically unchanged; the country still "adheres to the general policy of taking agriculture as the foundation and industry as the leading factor." The seven goals for 1964 include, above all, a better harvest; a steady rise in industrial production; greater investment in basic industries and farm irrigation projects; more efficient management and higher productivity; a smoother flow of goods between town and country; and an "appropriate" rise in living standards. In a drive to show that even in China, with its age-old history of natural disasters, man's ingenuity and labour can create defences against acts of God, agricultural investment is to be concentrated in selected areas.

For the present, then, policy acknowledges the need to foster agriculture if investment in industry is to be raised. Whether this commonsense view would prevail after another good harvest or two is a matter for conjecture; in these circumstances the Chinese authorities might be tempted once again into believing that the country's resources were adequate to sustain a breakneck growth rate. (This and the major problems confronting the economy will be discussed in the last chapter). By their boldness the Chinese leaders have certainly pulled their country out of a dire crisis, for the greater part admittedly of their own making. 1962 was a less bad year than 1961; at the very least, branches of light industry relying on non-agricultural raw materials did better than in 1961 and, according to the Peking People's Daily editorial of 2nd January 1963, there was "striking progress in readjustment" and the capacity of "numerous industrial and mining enterprises built in earlier years was coming into fuller use."

A year later the same paper characterized 1963 as a "year of brilliant success" with targets fulfilled or overfulfilled and a great improvement in the range and quality of goods available. There is a measure of truth in this self-congratulation; production undoubtedly rose, and by the end of the year consumer goods were much more freely available while prices dropped. But neither 1962 nor 1963 yielded more than an average harvest, and for the foreseeable future agricultural performance determines the pace of growth. One might hazard a guess that the present level of output is not greatly, if at all, in excess of that

of the best pre-disaster year; but an above-average harvest in 1964
would give the opportunity to bring into full use the industrial capacity
that has been rationalized during the last two years.

CHAPTER **3** TRADE TRENDS
AND
POLICIES

ORGANIZATION AND CONTROL

The Communist Government set out to control foreign trade as
energetically as it set out to control the rest of the economy. The
foreign merchants were quickly ousted and the private element was
disposed of soon after. Already during the war against Japan, the
government had assumed a major role in foreign trade and though,
so long as the Kuomintang regime lasted, foreigners hoped to regain
at least part of their one-time share in China trade, the Communists'
victory soon demonstrated that this was not to be. Except in the case
of Japanese firms, which were nationalized at the end of the war,
foreign interests were edged out by means of regulations: for example,
forbidding payment of dividends, controlling markets and sources of
supply, laying down onerous conditions regarding the hiring and
firing of labour, restricting credit and the free use of bank balances.
The compradores, too, the middlemen of prewar days between the
foreign merchants and the Chinese business community, were an
early target of the government and only those who were prepared
to act on behalf of the State Corporations have been able to continue
in operation. In 1950, private interests still handled nearly a third
of the total volume of trade, but by 1954 they had less than 2 per cent.

As in other Communist countries, a number of State Corporations
was set up, each handling the import and export of a specific range of
goods or dealing with some other aspect of trade, such as shipping.
All trade negotiations are normally conducted through these corporations, with the commercial departments of permanent diplomatic
missions abroad holding only a watching brief. Members of many of
the corporations spend a good deal of their time travelling, and
representatives of certain of them are more or less permanently
posted in important centres; for example, the China National Machinery Import Corporation is well represented in Western Europe and
Sinofracht Ship Chartering and Broking Corporation has officers in
London. The Ministry of Foreign Trade, set up in 1952 when the
former Ministry of Trade was split and its functions relating to
domestic distribution handed to the Ministry of Internal Commerce,
controls the activities of the corporations and generally supervises

external trade. Through the Foreign Trade Control Office, the
government can validate or cancel any individual export or import
transaction and determine the price at which any purchase or sale
is made.

Foreign trade has always been an integral part of the government's
general economic plans, whether annual or long-term, and during the
years of rehabilitation the authorities set themselves two objectives:
to reduce and eventually eliminate the deficit and to evolve a system
of trade regulation geared to the country's economic development.
The Common Programme's attitude to the matter was somewhat
defensive, a reaction perhaps to the dominance of the foreign merchant in prewar years; it stated that legitimate foreign trade would
be protected but that "control of foreign trade shall be enforced" and
that domestic industry would be shielded from foreign competition.
A more positive approach was, however, soon adopted and in a report
on China's trade for 1954 the Minister, Yeh Chi-chuang, reduced the
matter to its simplest terms: "the purpose of exporting is for importing, which in turn is for the sake of the country's industrialization".
It is therefore hardly surprising that there is a close correlation
between the development of the economy described in the previous
chapter and the development of foreign trade; a detailed analysis of
Russia's exports to China in the 'fifties would tell a great part of
the story of the latter's industrialization during the first ten years of
the Communist regime. External factors, however, acted as signi-
ficantly on foreign trade as internal ones and the rhythm of trade
development is thus not exactly parallel with that of the internal
economy. But 1957, which saw the end of the First Five-Year Plan,
was also a watershed for external trade, since in that year the sting
was taken out of the embargo on China trade when the United Kingdom
decided to apply one set of strategic controls to trade with all
Communist countries.

THE STATISTICAL PROBLEM

While the Chinese authorities early recognized the importance of
foreign trade, they never published detailed trade statistics, despite
the fact that trade was one of the few subjects that had been fully
documented before the war and for which the apparatus of data collection already existed. It is technically possible to build up from
the absolute and percentage figures sporadically released a statistical
series of imports and exports from the Chinese side for at least the
years 1950 to 1958. It is doubtful, however, whether it is worth the
trouble involved in attempting to justify a reconciliation of so many

often inconsistent figures to arrive at so limited a result, which in any
case cannot be translated into terms of an internationally recognized
currency. No adequate data are available from Chinese sources on the
composition or direction of trade nor on the matter of payments. For
the record, it may be noted that Ten Great Years, the only compre-
hensive statistical survey of the People's Republic available in English,
devotes two tables to foreign trade. The first shows the total volume
of trade turnover rising from 4.2 billion yuan in 1950 to 12.9 billion
yuan in 1958 with the pattern of annual increases as follows (per cent):

1951	+43.2	1955	+29.6
1952	+ 8.6	1956	- 1.1
1953	+25.2	1957	- 3.8
1954	+ 4.7	1958	+23.2

The second table shows the "volume of import and export trade by
category".

VOLUME OF TRADE

| Percentages | Imports | | Exports | | |
	Capital goods	Consumer goods	Industrial & mining products	Processed agricultural products[a]	Other agricultural products[a]
1950	87.2	12.8	9.3	33.2	57.5
1953	93.0	7.0	18.4	25.9	55.7
1957	92.7	7.3	28.4	31.5	40.1
1958	93.7	6.3	27.5	37.0	35.5

a. Including the products of "side occupations".

Source SSB, Ten Great Years.

While the definitions of the categories have no doubt been stretched
to emphasize to the utmost the picture that it is desired to create, of
no inessential imports and a growing volume of processed exports,
there seems little reason to suppose that the figures do not reflect

what was taking place in those years. But they are not very informative and they leave unexplained some important points, as, for example what exactly is meant by volume in this context.

The alternative of analysing and assessing China's trade from partners' returns is open to many and serious objections; but it is possible to take the measure of most of these, and the method has the virtue of bringing considerable enlightenment. In this and the following chapter, therefore, it is the partners' figures that are used; but when trying to assess China's total trade in this way the following factors must be borne in mind:

1. The coverage will be incomplete. The omissions are, however, unlikely to be very important.

2. Certain countries, particularly in the earlier years and mainly in Western Europe, failed to distinguish between trade with China and trade with Taiwan. Some even included Hong Kong under China. This, unavoidably, tends to exaggerate the level of China trade.

3. An export recorded in Europe in one year may not be recorded as a Chinese import until the following year, and vice versa. Hence derived trade statistics cannot reflect the position in any one year accurately.

4. Lastly, and most importantly, figures taken to represent China's imports are in fact the partner's exports f.o.b., while China's exports are others' imports c.i.f. Thus no allowance is made for China paying insurance and freight, while it is credited with receipts on these accounts which it has not earned. Thus if no adjustment is made, balances in favour of China are overstated and adverse balances understated.

For those who have not the time to scrutinize the trade statistics of each individual partner over a decade or so and to extract the details of trade with China, there are two major short cuts: the United Nations in its Yearbook of International Trade and quarterly Direction of International Trade provides statistics of most countries' trade with China, while the U.S. Department of Commerce compiles data on free world trade with the Sino-Soviet Bloc in its annual reports to Congress under the Mutual Defense Assistance Control Act of 1951. In the statistical appendix to the present monograph and throughout the text, the U.N. figures have been used, supplemented, particularly in the later years, by data from countries' own trade statistics. It will, however, be as well to admit at the outset that no two sources

will necessarily agree to within $100 million or so on China's global
trade, and individual sources do not always remain internally consistent over a period of years. This is to be regretted, but it is doubtful whether the results would repay great expenditure of time in
striving to refine to the utmost what must remain estimates. The
figures in this monograph for the most part represent orders of
magnitude, except when individual countries' trade statistics are
being analysed.

KOREA AND THE EMBARGO

The Communists' first step in relation to foreign trade was to set
up the kind of control mechanism adopted by most countries in balance-
of-payments difficulties. All trade was subjected to licence, imports
were divided into four categories ranging from essentials to luxuries,
whose purchase was prohibited, and the Bank of China was given control
over all dealings in foreign exchange. By dint of an extremely stringent
import policy and by maximizing exports, a surplus was achieved in
1950 and hailed as a triumph for Communist planning. Elation was,
however, abruptly terminated by the outbreak of the Korean war and
the subsequent Chinese intervention. When it became apparent that
this latter move would entail sanctions by the non-Communist world,
the Chinese authorities, not yet confident that they could obtain the
supplies that they required from the Soviet Bloc, stepped up purchases
from the West and imports once again surged ahead of exports. One
estimate of the value of trade in 1949-52 is quoted below; other
figures have been adduced by other authorities, but the trend shown
in the table is generally accepted.

VALUE OF TRADE 1949-1952

$ million	Imports	Exports	Balance
1949	179	165	− 14
1950	436	466	+ 30
1951	1,033	672	− 361
1952	717	478	− 239

Source Y.L. Wu, An Economic Survey of Communist China.

In 1950, the Communist Bloc provided a fifth of China's imports and took rather less than a third of China's exports; by 1952 it was supplying over two-thirds of imports and taking not far short of three-quarters of all exports. Although some shift in trade in this direction would certainly have taken place on ideological grounds, the sudden and swift swing of the pendulum was occasioned by the U.N. embargo on trade with China. On May 18, 1951, the General Assembly re-commended that all nations apply an embargo to Communist China and North Korea covering "arms, ammunition, and implements of war, atomic energy materials, petroleum, transportation materials of strategic value and items useful in the production of arms, ammunition and the implements of war." Already in December 1950 when China entered the war, the United States had prohibited all exports to the mainland - a prohibition that remains in force in 1964 - though it continued to import significant quantities of strategic goods of Chinese origin for stockpiling until 1953. Most other non-Communist countries willingly complied with the U.N. directive while the Korean war lasted and restricted their trade with China to such non-strategic items as cotton, fertilizer, textiles, textile machinery, dyes, drugs etc. With the ending of the war, however, restrictions became increasingly irksome to a number of countries and agitation for reform and relaxation grew.

The first major crack in the wall came when Ceylon, in the face of strong U.S. disapproval, agreed to exchange rubber against Chinese rice. Pressure for general reform mounted in the Consultative Committee and its subordinate Coordinating Committee (COCOM). This body was set up in Paris in 1949 on a voluntary basis by a number of Western countries to control strategic exports to the European Soviet Bloc, and was also given the task of coordinat-ing measures to limit trade with China (CHINCOM). Although no other country followed the United States lead in prohibiting trade with China, CHINCOM lists were much longer than COCOM lists. As the Korean war receded, the logic of this became less apparent to countries heavily dependent on foreign trade for their prosperity, who saw in China a potentially valuable market - a view encouraged and embellished by the Chinese authorities. In addition, the cost and trouble of administering two embargo lists were coming to be regarded as out of all proportion to the results achieved, particularly as the Eastern European countries could and did re-export to China goods of Western European origin that appeared on the CHINCOM but not on the COCOM list. Unanimity of view on the revision of the CHINCOM list was unattainable; and eventually, after years of fruitless dis-cussion, the United Kingdom resolved the deadlock in May 1957 by announcing that it would apply the COCOM list of strategic goods in trade with China. Despite U.S. opposition, other countries followed

this lead, and with the subsequent revisions to the single list, the
controls cannot now be considered as a significant hindrance to trade
between the free world and the Communists, except in the matter of
supplies that have a direct bearing on military potential.

Until 1957, however, the embargo was a very important factor
in trade; and as well as trying to circumvent it, China fought to
make it as uncomfortable as possible for those who operated it.
When, in March 1951, the Chinese Government introduced the barter
trade control regulations, it was decided that trade with the
Communists and 'neutrals' should be enlarged to the greatest possible
extent, while that with the capitalist world should be continued within
the limitations of the embargo (whose imposition was by that time a
certainty), with strategic goods in the Chinese sense (i.e. scarce
metals such as tungsten and antimony) being exchanged only for vital
imports unobtainable elsewhere or against less essential goods. It
was also decided to avoid maintaining or building up assets abroad
that might be frozen without warning or redress should the United
States convince its allies of the rightness of its own policy towards
the Communist regime. Following from this, the normal methods
of commercial trading and financing were abandoned in favour of one
or other type of barter deal where exports were permitted only
against virtually assured imports and any balances which accumulated were small and short-term. As a result of this policy, trade
with Western Europe appears to have been more or less in balance
in the years 1953-55. Then, as now, Asia was the principal milch
cow providing surpluses to pay for imports – at that time of
machinery and equipment from Eastern Europe.

THE GROWTH OF TRADE 1952-1961

Despite the importance of foreign trade in planning, the First
Five-Year plan contains little useful information on the subject. It
confirms the general pattern of trade laid down in 1951:

Trade with the Soviet Union and the People's Democracies, and
particularly our trade with the Soviet Union, form a solid foundation for fulfilment of our export and import task in these five
years and for ensuring normal growth of our foreign trade. It
is of the utmost significance for the development of our country.
This type of economic cooperation will enable us ...... to
obtain immense aid from the Soviet Union in the form of superb
technique and guarantee imports of equipment and materials
necessary for our Socialist industrialization. (It) will also enable

us to bring about a steady increase in our export trade ...... In
keeping with our peaceful foreign policy, and in accordance with
the principle of equality and mutual benefit, we should expand trade
with the countries of South East Asia. At the same time on condi-
tion that it benefits our socialist economic construction we should
continue to develop trade with other capitalist countries to increase
imports of certain necessary materials.[1]

The Plan also recommends that China familiarize itself with conditions in world markets, maximize production of export goods, and
improve the organization of the export trade; raise exports of major
agricultural products, minerals, handicrafts and certain (unspecified)
industrial goods; extend the range and improve the quality of exports;
implement the terms of trade contracts strictly, in cases of conflict
of interest giving exports priority over the home market; economize
the use of foreign exchange, and generally raise the efficiency of trade
organizations.

The only figure that the plan mentions is that the total volume of
trade turnover should rise by two-thirds between 1952 and 1957. If
Ten Great Years is to be believed, an increase of 70 per cent in
turnover was achieved between 1952 and 1955; but with the setbacks
in trade in 1956 and 1957, turnover in the latter year was only 62 per
cent higher than in 1952. The U.N. calculations given in the table
overleaf show a rise of 55 per cent in the value of turnover between
1952 and 1957, and one of 60 per cent between 1952 and 1956, the
peak year in their series. It must be remembered, however, that
the U.N. figures exclude trade with North Korea, North Vietnam
and Mongolia,which would be covered by the Chinese figures.

The U.N. calculations give a broad picture of China's trade from
1952 to 1961, the latest year for which it is possible to estimate the
total. Although the data have been taken from partners' returns,
they have been adjusted to include insurance and freight for imports
i.e. exports to China valued f.o.b., and vice versa. In addition,
they include estimates for countries either not listed separately or
for which full data are not available. For these reasons they are not
directly comparable with the figures shown in Appendix 3, which are
partner countries' import and export data unadjusted.

The deficits of earlier years were covered largely by Russian
loans and trade credit, and were incurred in importing machinery
and equipment for the First Plan. After rising by a fifth between
1952 and 1953, the first year of the Plan, imports grew more slowly

---

1. First Five-Year plan for Development of the National Economy
of the People's Republic of China.

during the next three years - by 6 per cent annually, that is by a
further fifth over the whole period. In 1957 they dropped by 7 per cent
with the exhaustion of the second Soviet loan (exports from the U.S.S.R.
to China fell from $733 million in 1956 to only $544 million in 1957),
before bounding ahead by nearly a third in 1958 under the influence of
the Great Leap spirit and the relaxation of the Western embargo.
Western Europe's exports to China rose from $230 million in 1957 to
$440 million in 1958, and Japan's too would have risen markedly but
for the Chinese Government's high-handed suspension of trade in May
1958. Although 1959 brought the first calamitous harvest and the
beginnings of the crisis, it was still possible to raise the general
level of trade in that year; but in 1960, 1961 and 1962 both imports
and exports shrank, the latter less drastically than the former since
debts to the Soviet Union and Eastern Europe were being repaid.
Trade appears to have moved on to a slightly higher plane in 1963
and the last two years may have yielded an export surplus.

CHINA'S TRADE 1952-1961

$ million	Imports	Exports	Balance
1952[a]	1,120	950	-170
1953	1,340	1,130	-210
1954	1,460	1,200	-260
1955	1,480	1,420	- 60
1956	1,620	1,700	+ 80
1957	1,510	1,700	+190
1958	1,980	1,970	+ 10
1959	2,180	2,210	+ 30
1960	2,090	2,040	- 50
1961	1,570	1,520	- 50

a. This year is included as a salutary reminder of the unwisdom
of marrying series of statistics on China's trade compiled by
different sources; cf table on page 30.

Source U.N. Yearbook of International Trade Statistics, 1961.

The progress of exports during the 'fifties shows clearly how
heavily dependent the country still is on agriculture. In the ten years,
exports spurted ahead on three occasions. In 1953 they were 19 per
cent up on 1952; the grain and cotton harvests of 1952 and 1953 were
well above those of the previous two years. 1955 and 1956 saw export

increases of 27 per cent and 20 per cent respectively; in this instance
the bumper 1955 harvest came at a time when industrial production
was beginning to benefit from investment in rationalization and new
capacity made during the years of rehabilitation and the first years
of the Plan. The 1958 and 1959 increases (of 16 per cent and 12 per
cent) were again the result of the coincidence of an excellent harvest
with the coming into operation of new industrial capacity - many of
the plants built with Soviet help were by then in production - which
extended the range of manufactured goods available for export.

The changes which have taken place in the composition of trade
emerge more clearly in the following chapter where trade with
individual partners is analysed. Exports have changed their character much less than have imports; agricultural and mineral products
still provide the greater part of foreign exchange earnings, though
textiles and manufactured consumer goods are sold extensively in
South East Asia and to the Eastern Bloc. Ironically enough, in the
early days of the regime when (if official estimates are to be believed)
harvests were still extremely small, China became for the first time
a net exporter of foodstuffs, mainly of rice and other foodgrains to
India; though rice is still exported, in particular to Ceylon in
exchange for rubber, it is no longer mainly of Chinese origin but
is obtained in triangular deals, involving for example Burma.

In the 'thirties machinery made up less than 10 per cent of the
import bill, but during the First Five-Year Plan about 60 per cent
of imports consisted of machinery and equipment while a further
30 per cent was basic materials for industry and agriculture. Of
this perhaps a third was metals; other important items included
fertilizers, high-grade seed and breeding stock, liquid fuels. The
ten per cent left over for consumer goods covered, among other
things, drugs, kerosene and sugar. The heavy food imports of the
last three years will have distorted the pattern somewhat, but insufficient data are yet to hand to judge the matter fairly.

DIRECTION AND BALANCE

It is possible to get a more precise picture of the direction
than of the composition of trade. As the table on the following page
shows, reliance on the Eastern Bloc had already passed its zenith
before the end of the first plan and by 1957 the area's share in
China's trade had dropped to two-thirds (this was still an enormous
proportion compared with the prewar share). The pendulum
started to swing back in favour of the non-Communist world for
a number of reasons. In the first place, by 1956 the amount of

DIRECTION OF CHINA'S POSTWAR TRADE[a]

		1953		1957		1958		1959		1961	
		Exports	Imports	Exports	Imports	Exports	Imports	Exports	Imports	Exports	Imports
Total	$ mn	1,130	1,340	1,700	1,510	1,970	1,980	2,210	2,180	1,520	1,570
	%	100	100	100	100	100	100	100	100	100	100[c]
N. & S. America	$ mn	13	1	8	6	8	19	7	5	12[b]	200[c]
	%	1	-	-	-	-	1	-	-	-	13
W. Europe	$ mn	120	81	135	200	170	440	205	390	185	190
	%	11	6	8	13	9	22	9	18	12	12
U.S.S.R. & E. Europe	$ mn	725	1,080	1,120	1,010	1,295	1,220	1,600	1,520	925	810
	%	64	81	66	67	66	62	72	70	61	52
Asia & Middle East	$ mn	254	175	407	256	460	253	381	211	375	187
	%	22	13	24	17	23	13	17	10	25	12
Others	$ mn	18	3	30	38	37	48	27	54	23	183[c]
	%	2	-	2	3	2	2	1	2	2	12

a. Estimates based largely on import data of trading partners. Where exports to China (Taiwan) could not be separately distinguished they were shown as exports to China (mainland). Exports to Mongolia, N. Korea and N. Vietnam are included under this heading. The inter-trade of these countries and their trade with China (mainland) are excluded. b. Estimate. c. 1961 saw the first big shipments of grain from Canada and Australia to China. Note: percentages may not add to 100 owing to rounding.

Source U.N. Yearbook of International Trade Statistics, 1961, published 1963.

the Soviet loan still available was shrinking rapidly and in 1957 it was
exhausted; repayment of the first loan started in 1954.   Secondly,
there is reason to suppose that China became dissatisfied with the
terms that it was obtaining in trade with the U.S.S.R. and its
satellites; there is circumstantial evidence that it was paying high
for imported machinery and getting in return an unfavourable price
for its agricultural goods and raw materials.   Thirdly, the grip of the
embargo was loosening.   Although there was no question of China
deliberately reverting to traditional partners, if imports were to be
paid for on the nail it was most advantageous to obtain them from the
cheapest sources; and both Western Europe and Japan were potentially, and in some respects actually, at least as attractive suppliers
as the Eastern Bloc.   In 1958 and 1959, however, the absolute level
of exchanges with the European Communists continued to rise, and
in 1959 the proportion rose again following a very sharp increase in
trade with the U.S.S.R., whose exports of machinery and equipment to China increased from $318 million in 1958 to $598 million
in 1959, nearly all of this being accounted for by sales of complete
plant, up from $166 million in 1958 to $400 million in 1959.   The
real setback came in 1960 when the ideological quarrel flared up
and the Soviet experts were withdrawn from China.   Sino-Soviet trade
turnover dropped from $2,055 million in 1959 to $750 million in 1962.

Although initially the Communist Bloc's loss promised to be the
gain of Western Europe and Japan, the economic crisis that followed
the Great Leap so reduced the level of trade and necessitated such
huge expenditure on imported foodstuffs that Western European exports
to China fell steadily from the 1958 peak of $400 million to around
$150 million in 1962.   1963, for which full figures are not yet avail-
able, probably brought a recovery to around $180 million.   In the
short term, the beneficiaries were Canada and Australia.

In the postwar years trade with the Communist Bloc has not
merely absorbed all the share held by the United States before the
war, but has taken much that was once Japanese.   In 1938, Asia
accounted for nearly 70 per cent of China's imports and took some
60 per cent of its exports: since the war the figures have been
nearer to 15 per cent and 20 per cent respectively.   Before the
annexation of Manchuria, Japan alone provided a fifth or more of
China's imports and took a quarter or so of its exports; even after
Manchoukuo had been established as a separate puppet state, Japan
was responsible for about 15 per cent of both China's imports and
exports.   Japan has not yet re-established its position in China
trade and hitherto the Chinese Government has seen Asia as an
area where certain vital raw materials must be bought, but where -
equally important - a trade surplus can be earned through sales
of textiles, consumer and light industrial goods, and such products

as cement. The continued existence of Hong Kong assures an unfailing sterling surplus, for the Colony must buy much of what it needs in China yet has little to sell there in return. Malaya is another source of sterling and surpluses are also often earned in trade with Ceylon, Burma and Indonesia, though at least part of China's exports there are aid-financed.

TRADE BALANCES BY AREA

$ million	U.S.S.R. and E. Europe	Western Europe	Asia	Total including others
1953	−355	+ 39	+ 79	−210
1954	−340	+ 20	+ 48	−260
1955	−225	+ 28	+ 128	− 60
1956	− 95	− 20	+ 194	+ 80
1957	+110	− 65	+ 151	+190
1958	+ 75	−270	+ 225	+ 10
1959	+ 80	−185	+ 170	+ 30
1960	− 20	−145	+ 188	− 50
1961	+115	− 5	+ 188	− 50
1953−61	−655	−603	+1,371	−320

Source U.N. Statistical Yearbook, 1962.

Over the nine years the surplus on trade with Asia covered the combined deficit on trade with the U.S.S.R. and Western Europe, with something to spare towards the deficit with minor partners and with recent food suppliers such as Canada and Australia.

CHINA'S BALANCE OF PAYMENTS

With data on trade so scanty it is hardly surprising that information from the Chinese side on international payments is wholly lacking. In the circumstances, there seems little point in attempting to draw up a detailed account and quantify individual items, but it will be useful to consider the general pattern of the balance of payments. If yet another adjustment were made to the figures in the table on page 36, to bring imports on to an f.o.b. basis, the balance of trade

as normally defined in balance-of-payments calculations would be in
China's favour. As against this, insurance and freight would be net
debit items. Another current debit item is the servicing of Russian
loans; although the sum involved may not be large it is certainly not
offset by the minuscule interest which China receives on the loans
that it extends itself.

The size of the freight bill is a cause of some concern to the
Chinese authorities, and they have tried to reduce it by various
means. When trade with the West began to expand in 1958, China
started to charter substantial quantities of shipping on the Baltic
Exchange and elsewhere, and has continued to do so ever since,
presumably finding this cheaper than having cargo carried by the
lines serving the Far East. It has also bought ships from Poland
and East Germany, and in 1956, 1957 and 1958 it purchased a
number of wartime Liberty ships. Less successfully, it has
launched one or two small ships built in Chinese yards. A merchant
fleet may be assembled slowly, but it seems rather unlikely to be
a high-priority item for the time being. Some trade with the Soviet
Union and Eastern Europe is, of course, carried overland and rail
connections with the U.S.S.R. have been substantially improved.
In 1962 a joint-stock shipping company was set up in cooperation
with Albania to carry trade between the two countries - a service
apparently unattractive to either West or East.

The balance of expenditure by Chinese abroad and by foreigners
in China is a good deal less important now than before the war, though
there was a substantial exchange of personnel with the Soviet Union
and Eastern Europe in the hey-day of cooperation; but so little is
known about the manner in which it was accounted for that it is
impossible to say how it affected the balance of payments. A prop of
prewar payments that is, however, still of great importance is
remittances by Overseas Chinese. While the important Chinese
group in the United States has not been able to remit directly to
China since the Communists came to power, there are still many
Chinese in Hong Kong and South East Asia who send money to their
relatives at home. Most of it passes through the Bank of China in
Hong Kong, but some may be transmitted direct from Singapore.
Three Overseas Chinese banks maintain offices in Shanghai: the
Overseas Chinese Banking Corporation (incorporated in Singapore),
the Bank of East Asia and the Chi-Yu Bank. The extent of the remittances is a matter of guesswork and they almost certainly vary a good
deal from year to year, depending partly on events in China, partly
on the prosperity of the emigrants' adopted countries. Hong Kong
sources estimate the flow in a normal year at around $100 million,
but in some years the figure may fall as low as $40 million.

There is no doubt that the Chinese set great store by this source

of income and are prepared to compromise with their Marxist principles in order to tap it more fully. The money is either sent in the
form of cash to relatives or invested in Overseas Chinese Investment
Corporations set up by the authorities in areas that experienced heavy
emigration in the past. The Corporations channel their funds into
projects such as sugar, ramie or paper mills, canneries and oil
presses and, under regulations promulgated in 1957, are permitted
to pay dividends of up to 8 per cent, half of which supposedly may be
transmitted abroad provided that the Bank of China's permission is
obtained for each transaction. The share capital remains the property
of the investor, who can either collect it, after twelve years, in
Chinese currency or reinvest it. More recently, Overseas Chinese
have been given the opportunity to buy houses, which will remain
their private property, through the Shanghai Overseas Chinese Investment Company. During the food crisis new ways of attracting small
cash remittances were devised and a good deal of ingenuity was dis-
played in converting emigrants' sympathy for their starving relatives
into foreign exchange. Quite a trade developed in the export from
Hong Kong to China of food parcels, whose contents originated in
China, against payment of duties in foreign exchange.

These normal current earnings were, however, insufficient to
balance a capital account that, since 1956 or 1957, had been almost
wholly made up of negative items; for on this side of the balance
sheet, too, any repayment of Chinese loans that may have taken
place has been much more than offset by amortization of Soviet
loans, both economic and military, to China.[2] In addition, in most
years China extended some new aid abroad, though much of it was
in the form of trade credits. In 1959, therefore, for the first time
since the years immediately before the Communists came to power,
China began to sell silver in London (small sales to Germany had
been made in the previous year). In 1959 itself offerings were small;

---

2. It is convenient in discussing the balance of payments to refer
to the capital account in the normal western terminology. In fact,
however, Russian aid to China rarely involved the extension of
credits which were then drawn down over a period of time and
whose utilisation would properly be recorded in the capital account
year by year. It appears that normally the U.S.S.R. despatched
specific goods or provided specific services, and was subsequently
repaid in specific goods. These flows are recorded in value terms
in the trade and current payments accounts for the year in which they
occurred; an equivalent entry is necessary on the capital account to
'balance' out.

the London market took some 2.6 million troy ounces worth about
$1.5 million. The amount rose sharply to 7.4 million ounces in
1960 and 46.4 million ounces in 1961, before dropping to 25.7 million
ounces in 1962; no sales were made in 1963, though delivery of
290,000 ounces sold in 1962 was not made until the first quarter of
the year. In all, more than $50 million worth was sold in London
during the four years. The abrupt termination of sales remains
something of a mystery, particularly since the price on the London
market averaged 110.1264 pence per ounce in 1963 against 91.5103
in 1962 and only 80.2252 in 1961. Stocks based mainly on coin –
there is little new production in China – may have been nearing
exhaustion or the immediate need for foreign exchange may have
been satisfied; possibly it was judged unwise to convert more of
the metal into foreign exchange despite the attractive price.

In 1961 China also made a solitary excursion into the London
gold market and the metal was accepted as 'good delivery'; 35,997
troy ounces-fine was sold. Some may also have been sold about
this time in Hong Kong. Gold has almost certainly been used on
occasion in partial settlement of debts to the Soviet Union – it
was explicitly mentioned as one of the means of repaying the first
Soviet loan – and it may at some future date be used in settlements
with Western countries. Unlike silver, the metal is produced in
China, though it is not known whether new prospecting has raised
output above the rather meagre prewar levels. However, there
have from time to time been reports of rising production, particularly in the Tsaidam basin.

The size of foreign exchange holdings is not calculable and
probably not very important. The authorities would be most unlikely
to build up foreign currency balances beyond their current requirements and they are in no position to run up excessive debts; apart
from normal short-term trade credit, there are a few deals on
eighteen months to two year deferred terms, mainly with the Japanese, the Canadians and the Australians, and the longer-term five-
year credits covering the recently negotiated purchases of complete
plant from Western Europe and Japan. On the basis of past ex-
perience, it seems probable that these commitments will be met
punctiliously and that foreign trade will continue to be so managed
that exchanges are maintained at the highest level consistent with
the resources at the Chinese Government's disposal – though it
would not be surprising if a quite substantial gold holding were built
up for use in emergencies to avoid a repetition of the disastrous fall
in trade which occurred in the early 'sixties. Short-term deficits
can be covered by drawing on the sterling balances that are normally
used to finance China's trade with the free world.

CHAPTER 4   TRADE WITH WHOM?

THE RUSSIAN GIANT

In the ten years from 1951 to 1960 the U.S.S.R. and Eastern
Europe accounted annually for two-thirds or more of China's trade
turnover, the Soviet Union alone being responsible for nearly 50 per
cent in 1959 and having an average share of over 40 per cent in the
years 1957-60.

In 1949 the U.S.S.R. signed various agreements with Chinese
Regional Governments for the exchange of Russian industrial equipment against foodstuffs, but the story of postwar Sino-Soviet trade
starts with the agreements of February and April 1950 made with
the Central Government in Peking. The first extended a credit (see
below); the second provided for the barter of Chinese tungsten, antimony, coal, soya beans, peanuts, silk, tea, bristles, furs and hides
against Soviet industrial material and equipment (two-thirds of the
total); railway and communications equipment; agricultural machinery;
breeding stock, seeds, newsprint, kerosene, and medicines. Similar
trade protocols have been signed annually ever since, usually in March
or April; a long-term trade agreement believed to be under negotiation early in 1960 must have foundered on the rocks of Sino-Soviet
ideological differences.

In the early years the details of the protocols were not always
released and in the absence of trade statistics from either partner
(the U.S.S.R. only started to issue annual trade statistics in 1955)
it is not possible to itemize the goods being exchanged, but industrial
equipment will certainly have continued to be the major Soviet export.
From 1955 to 1960 the countries were less secretive about what they
intended to exchange and normally indicated that trade was expected
to rise by a certain percentage; in the last three years, however, the
protocols have again become less informative and there has been a
conspicuous absence of reference to the volume of trade to be attained.
In view of the drastic decline in the value of trade since 1959, this is
hardly surprising.

On the known figures, the Soviet Union was in debt to China on the
trade account to the tune of $167 million over the thirteen years but
much of this might disappear if the balance of trade in 1951 were

known, leaving only a small Chinese surplus, if any at all, to set off
against other obligations to Russia.[1].

SINO-SOVIET TRADE

$ million	Soviet Exports	Imports	Balance
1950	388	188	+200
1952	554	414	+140
1953	697	475	+222
1954	826	545	+281
1955	748	644	+104
1956	733	764	- 31
1957	544	738	-194
1958	635	881	-246
1959	955	1,100	-145
1960	817	848	- 31
1961	367	552	-185
1962	234	516	-282

Note: Figures for 1951 are not available.

Sources 1950-52 - E.S. Kirby (ed), Contemporary China III, 1958-59;
1953-54 - United Nations op.cit.; 1955-62 - Soviet Trade Statistics.

These obligations include military aid to an unknown and probably
substantial amount provided during the Korean war and a long-term
credit - again of unknown value but perhaps amounting to something
over $400 million - established in 1955 and representing the value

---

1. It is just possible that commercial trade in that year may have
been greatly reduced because of military deliveries (which would
have been accounted for separately) and it may not have been
heavily to China's disadvantage. Quite apart from the capacity of
Russian industry, transport facilities would have been inadequate
to move large quantities of both war material and civil supplies.
On the basis of the figures quoted in the table above, China's
debt to Russia at the end of 1960 on trade account was $300 million
- a sum surprisingly close to the $320 million trade debts at end -
1960 (see page 46).

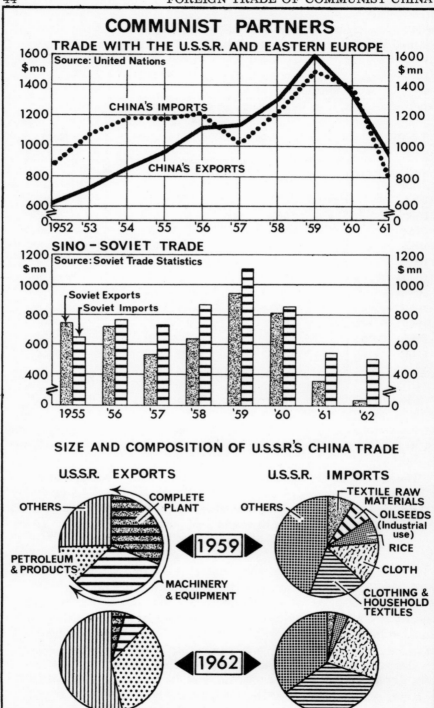

COMMUNIST PARTNERS

TRADE WITH THE U.S.S.R. AND EASTERN EUROPE

Source: United Nations

CHINA'S IMPORTS

CHINA'S EXPORTS

1952 '53 '54 '55 '56 '57 '58 '59 '60 '61

SINO - SOVIET TRADE

Source: Soviet Trade Statistics

Soviet Exports
Soviet Imports

1955 '56 '57 '58 '59 '60 '61 '62

SIZE AND COMPOSITION OF U.S.S.R.'S CHINA TRADE

U.S.S.R. EXPORTS

OTHERS

COMPLETE PLANT

PETROLEUM & PRODUCTS

MACHINERY & EQUIPMENT

1959

U.S.S.R. IMPORTS

TEXTILE RAW MATERIALS

OTHERS

OILSEEDS (Industrial use)

RICE

CLOTH

CLOTHING & HOUSEHOLD TEXTILES

1962

Source: Soviet Trade Statistics

of Soviet military supplies at the Port of Dairen and Soviet shares in
the mixed Soviet-Chinese companies, [2] both of which were handed
over to the Peking Government. Soviet aid proper, which as we have
already seen was not over-generous, is largely accounted for in the
trade statistics themselves since for the most part both supplies and
repayment were in kind. Only two long-term economic loans were
extended by the U.S.S.R.; the first, worth $300 million, was granted
in 1950; it carried 1 per cent interest and was repayable in annual
instalments of $30 million from 1954 through 1963 in raw materials,
gold and dollars. It was used principally to buy machinery and
equipment for the construction and rehabilitation of fifty specific
projects covering power plants, mines, railways etc; it was a
partial compensation for the Russian depredations in Manchuria
immediately after the war. The second loan, of $130 million, was
made in 1954 to finance basic industrial construction up to 1957.
It carried interest at 2 per cent per annum but the terms of repayment were never made known. It may, however, be surmised that
they required yearly deliveries of food and raw materials over a
period of perhaps five to ten years starting probably in 1958.
     For the rest, the Soviet Union from time to time committed
itself to delivering machinery for specific projects vital to Chinese
plants; but there was no element of credit in these deals, other
than short-term trade credit; they were made against counter-
deliveries of Chinese goods. Their value to the Chinese presumably lay in the fact that they enabled the authorities to plan ahead
in the knowledge that the machinery and know-how would be available
when the time came. Thus, in the autumn of 1953 help was promised
for 91 more large-scale projects in addition to the 50 covered by the
first loan; and in 1954 the total was raised to 156 projects, which
formed the nucleus of the First Five-Year Plan. In 1956 there was
a further increase of 55 (bringing the total to 211), calling for an
additional $625 million of Soviet goods. Of these, 140 were due to
be started and nearly 60 finished by the end of the First Plan in 1957.
In 1959 help was promised in undertaking another 78 projects in the
years 1959-67, with a Soviet commitment to supply $1.25 billion of
equipment to complement the plant and machinery being provided by
China itself.
     It is, however, in technical assistance more than physical supplies
that the help of the U.S.S.R. has been invaluable to China. The Sino-
Soviet Scientific and Technical Cooperation Commission set up in 1954

---

2. These were similar to the Soviet joint-stock companies set up in
Eastern Europe. In China they dealt mainly in mineral and petroleum
exploitation in Sinkiang, air transport and shipbuilding.

made available to the Chinese large numbers of blueprints for factories, power stations, etc., and working drawings for the installation and running of machines; it arranged for thousands of Chinese students and workers to study and train in the Soviet Union; it sent Russian experts to work in China. In the words of Edgar Snow: "China had to pay in exports of equal value for all the machines and technical help received, but free access to Soviet scientific and industrial knowledge, patents, blueprints and patterns saved her years of trial and error and incalculable amounts of time and money."[3] It is hardly surprising that the withdrawal of this help in mid-1960 added confusion to China's economy, already confounded by a disastrous harvest. The gravity of the matter was not immediately admitted on the Chinese side: indeed the subject tended to be brushed aside on the grounds that the experts who had been withdrawn had finished their work or that a mild tiff between friends was not a serious matter. However, by 1964 the Chinese Government was collecting every jot and tittle of evidence of Soviet perfidy, quoting figures of the withdrawal from China of 1,390 Soviet experts, the tearing up of 343 contracts, and the cancellation of 257 projects (some of which can have been no bigger than repair shops).

Already by 1961 the coolness in relations between the two countries was affecting the level of trade, but it did not prevent the Russians from offering, nor the Chinese from accepting, some meagre contributions towards easing the latter's dire economic plight. In the agreement signed that year the U.S.S.R. pledged itself to deliver 500,000 tons of sugar as an interest-free loan to be repaid in five years and agreed to phase repayment of outstanding trade debts of $320 million as follows: 1962, $9 million; 1963, $55 million; and 1964 and 1965 each $128 million. The surpluses which China earned on Soviet trade in both 1961 and 1962 were, in fact, set against this debt and a supplement to the 1963 trade protocol stated that with the surplus earned in that year the debt would be paid off ahead of schedule. It would thus appear that Chinese claims to be free of all debts to the U.S.S.R. by 1965 are well founded.

Commodity Trade Patterns

Soviet exports to China were at peak heights in 1954 and 1959 – the second year of the First Five-Year Plan and the second year of the Second Plan. Owing to lack of data it is impossible to examine the make-up of 1954 trade – but nearly one third by value of 1959 delivieries was accounted for by complete plants and a further third by machinery and equipment. Until 1962 these two items accounted

---

3. Edgar Snow, The Other Side of the River.

for the lion's share; no detail is given of the complete plants supplied but the remainder of the machinery and equipment is shown in fair detail (see Appendix 4, which lists the major items), and analysis throws interesting light on the type and timing of deliveries. Shipments of power plant, for example, doubled between 1958 and 1959 and remained large in 1960; 1959 exports were mainly of steam and diesel units, but in 1960 a 150MW hydrogenerator was supplied - the only one to be delivered of the eight promised for the great San Men dam project on the Yellow River. This failure to deliver will seriously delay the whole 23,000MW Yellow River scheme, once scheduled for completion in 1967. Oil-drilling equipment is another item of considerable importance to China that Russia has lately withheld; exports began to tail off in 1959 and ceased in 1962, but this has to some extent been offset by greater deliveries from Rumania. Soviet help in building up the iron and steel industry is not very apparent in the trade statistics, though $2.6 million worth of rolling mill equipment was supplied in 1955, the year in which work started on the Wuhan iron and steel works, probably the largest single project carried out with Soviet help. The continued large purchases of Soviet sheet steel and tubes rather give the lie to Chinese claims to near self-suffiency in steel.

Vehicles and agricultural machinery were large items in trade in 1958 to 1960 and might well have formed an increasing proportion of the total but for the breach. The jumpt in tractor imports in 1958 (2,656 to a value of $10.8 million were bought that year against only 68 in 1957 and 941 in 1959) probably reflects the Great Leap spirit, but may also have been designed to prepare the ground for the output of the Loyang tractor works (built with Russian help), which began operations in 1959 and was due to reach full annual capacity of 30,000 units in 1960. Truck imports were at a peak in 1958 and remained high in 1959 and 1960; railway rolling stock was bought in substantial quantity only in 1959, presumably because completion of new track mileage had outstripped the capacity of China's wagon and engine works. Railway freight turnover is officially reported to have risen from 60 billion ton/km in 1952 to 185 billion in 1958.

Road mileage in China is now put at some 270,000 miles, about five times the prewar length, and though most traffic is still non-mechanical the park of trucks, buses and automobiles has grown greatly. So, too, have the numbers of other users of petroleum and its products - industries, power plants, irrigation works, agricultural machinery. Very little is, however, known about the liquid fuel balance sheet. Two things only are certain: China's consumption remains pathetically small at less than 10 million tons a year, and the Soviet Union has played an important part in supplies. Rumania and Albania are also suppliers but the amounts involved are not known;

in Rumania's case as much as 1 million tons a year may have been shipped recently. China's own production of crude was only 300,000 tons in 1951, but in 1962 6 million tons was probably reached and there may have been a further rise in 1963, when China claimed to be able to make all the products required by the economy (though not necessarily in the quantities needed).

The cessation of exports of crude in 1961 was probably of no great consequence, though they were not entirely negligible in relation to Chinese orders of magnitude, but the cut in supplies of gasoline and diesel fuel in 1962 must have been very serious indeed. In that year Chinese refineries were instructed to step up output of products most needed in agriculture, for example light diesel fuels; and in 1963 there were reports of China trying to buy aviation spirit from Japan - but some grades remain on the embargo list.

China's exports to Russia fall broadly into three groups, metals, foodstuffs and agricultural raw materials, and textiles; and, apart from the tremendous drive to pay off debts that started in 1958-59, their most interesting feature is the startling change that took place in their composition between the first and the latest statistics published by the Russians, showing a massive shift to textiles and clothing. In 1955 oilseeds and edible oils supplied 20 per cent of the total, ores and metals 19 per cent, meat 11 per cent, textile raw materials 9 per cent and rice 6 per cent; in 1962 the percentages were nil, 12, nil, 3 and 4 respectively. Cloth meanwhile rose from 7 per cent to 14 in 1959 and 22 in 1962, clothing from 2 to 18 to 35.

Whose choice it was that the burden of repayment of outstanding obligations should fall on the textile sector is a matter for conjecture. The Russians have not been slow to take credit for doing the Chinese a favour by absorbing textile and light industrial goods that it might have been difficult to dispose of elsewhere, even, so it is claimed, at the expense of keeping some Soviet factories operating below capacity. But the Chinese goods must at least have provided welcome variety for the Soviet consumer at no great cost to the state. From the Chinese viewpoint, it was obviously advantageous to withhold from Russian trade as many as possible of those goods that were readily saleable to the capitalist world against foreign exchange with which to buy machinery and food, but the sudden upsurge in total exports to the U.S.S.R. was at least partly responsible for some uncomfortable moments in trade with western Europe, and the diversion of textiles and clothing westwards meant that the Chinese export drive in South East Asia begun in 1958 fizzled out without ever really getting up steam. It also meant that at a period when disaffection and disillusion with government policies were widespread and affecting the level of output, the domestic market could not be provided with consumer goods. However, on the assumption that they were faced with a peremptory demand to settle debts, the Chinese authorities seem to have hit on an efficient means of carrying out the unpleasant task comparatively painlessly to themselves without affording the Soviet Government much joy.

The ores exported by China to Russia are not specified in the Soviet trade statistics, but consist presumably of iron, manganese and chrome. Tin is the most important non-ferrous metal sent to the U.S.S.R.; shipments ranged from 22,000 tons in 1957 to 8,700 in 1962 and totalled 132,300 tons over the eight years for which statistics are available. The unit price fell sharply from $2825 a ton in 1955 to $2063 in 1956; it dropped again to $2000 in 1959 and $1964 in 1960 before recovering to $2000 in 1961 and 1962. Over those years the London price fluctuated from an average of £734.9 per (long) ton in 1958 to £896.5 in 1962 ($2025.6 per metric ton to $2471.0). Though the evidence is not conclusive, these figures do suggest that Russia was getting the Chinese metal cheap. It is worth noting that sales to Western Germany started to rise as those to the U.S.S.R. declined.

Rice shipments to Russia exceeded 150,000 tons every year from 1955 to 1962, with the exception of 1961, and in 1959 reached 658,400 tons. Sales of meat and edible vegetable oils were presumably suspended because of the agricultural crisis; there may also have been some diversion to non-Communist markets.

That old standby of Sino-Soviet trade, tea, continued to yield the equivalent of some $12 million to $15 million (nearly $20 million in 1959) a year until 1960, when it, too, fell victim to the ideological battle. China can have had no interest in curtailing deliveries; the initiative must have come from the Russians.

OTHER COMMUNIST PARTNERS

Trade with the other European countries within the Soviet orbit (with the exception of Poland) is less well documented statistically than that with the U.S.S.R. itself. The first barter agreements were signed with Czechoslovakia, Poland and East Germany in 1950, with Hungary in 1951 and with Bulgaria and Rumania in 1952. Until 1956 trade was conducted on the basis of annual barter or trade and payments agreements (with settlement in roubles); but in that year both East Germany and Czechoslovakia concluded long-term agreements (1957-62) to supply plant and equipment for the Second Chinese Five-Year Plan, and in 1958 and 1959 the other countries, with the exception of Rumania, concluded agreements covering the years to 1962, within the framework of which annual protocols were issued each year.

It was Russia's wish that China should seek full membership of the
Council for Mutual Economic Assistance (COMECON) and thus enable
Communist economic plans to be coordinated over an area extending
from the Elbe to the Yellow Sea; China, however, refused to become
more than an observer of Moscow's struggles to gain the Council's
acceptance for its views on the correct division of labour within the
Soviet Bloc. But the Peking Government seems to have succeeded in
Eastern Europe as it did in the U.S.S.R. in getting promises of
deliveries of machinery needed to carry out Chinese plans.

The annual protocols on trade with East European countries
normally list the goods to be exchanged and contain expressions of
intent to raise the volume of trade; in the early years the percentages
mentioned were substantial since trade started from negligible figures
but by 1963 only Rumania was proposing to do more business with
China. Eastern Europe's exports to China usually include machinery
and equipment (each country concentrating on its own special lines):
special steel; chemicals; precision instruments; rolling stock etc.
From 1954 to 1962 complete plant also figured in the export lists,
mainly those of the three north-eastern countries and also of Hungary,
which was the only country to continue including this item in 1963.
Chinese exports comprise: textiles, raw and processed; foodstuffs
and tea; non-ferrous metals; oilseeds and fats; and such traditional
items as bristles, feathers and tung oil.

East Germany was China's most important partner after the
U.S.S.R. largely, as in the Soviet instance, on account of deliveries
of complete plant. It was closely followed by Czechoslovakia, but
between 1960 and 1962 exchanges with that country contracted even
more sharply than those with the Soviet Union - possibly to the
relief of the Czech Government, faced with its own economic crisis.
Figures so far available for the recent past suggest that China is
engaged in settling all outstanding liabilities with the Bloc; exports
to both Poland and Czechoslovakia in 1962 were well above imports
from those countries and during 1963 China continued to earn a big
surplus on trade with Poland. Aid, in the normal sense of the term,
was not extended to China by the Bloc, though technical assistance
and the occasional gift of hospital equipment or the like was provided;
but China seems to have run up fairly big trade debts in 1958, when
East European deliveries rose by 44 per cent compared with the
previous year. 1960 and 1961, too, were deficit years.

A study of trade between China and Albania adds little to the story
of that bizarre friendship; so far as can be established total turnover
has never yet achieved $10 million a year and neither side chooses
to publish much statistical data. Not surprisingly, the balance is
consistently and heavily in China's favour, but this does not mean
that Albania has nothing that China wants: it has oil and chrome and

copper ores, though hardly in the requisite quantities. In the 1962
agreement China stated its intention to raise exports to Albania even
if this were not counterbalanced by greater Albanian shipments.
Although China gave aid to Albania as early as 1954 (see next chapter),
trade did not start until 1956 and it was not until after the 1957 Moscow
Conference that the friendship between the two began to ripen. By 1959
China still had less than 3 per cent of Albania's trade, Russia more
than 50 per cent; by 1962 the tables were fully turned and China had
60 per cent. Apart from the well-publicized grain shipments, China
provides Albania with steel, tyres, rubber, chemicals, drugs,
machinery and equipment and textiles.

Trade between China and its Asian Communist neighbours is the
least well-documented of the lot. Up to 1953 it was on a very small
scale indeed, but as rivalry with Moscow grew it became increasingly
necessary for Peking to make its presence felt. Mongolia has always
regarded Russia as the lesser of two evils (it is a member of COMECON)
and its shipments to China consist of small quantities of livestock and
animal products; it is an accidental victim of the shrinkage in Sino-
Soviet trade since at o ne time it earned a tidy income from transit
dues on the trains that daily traversed its territory. With North
Korea, Chinese trade is regulated by long-term agreements; the
first covered the years 1956-62, the current one extends from 1963
to 1967. North Korean exports consist mainly of fish, iron ore,
minerals and machinery (in the early days electricity, too, was sold
to China); North Vietnam in its turn sends hard coal, timber, jute,
chromite and agricultural produce; in exchange China provides among
other things steel, coal, machinery, tyres, chemicals, silk, fruit.
From the purely economic point of view, this is a most unprofitable
trading area.

WESTERN EUROPE

The Broad Pattern

The interest of Sino-West European trade lies in the future rather
than in the past so that the analysis of what has been can be much
shorter than in the case of the Soviet Union; speculation on what may
happen in coming years will be reserved as far as possible for the
last chapter. Even at its peak during the past decade, trade with
China accounted for only about one per cent of Western Europe's
exports and about one half of one per cent of its imports; China,
with more than twice the population, had a foreign trade turnover
in 1958 less than 5 per cent of that of Western Europe and by 1961
the figure had shrunk to under 3 per cent. Viewed from China's

angle, Western Europe was normally a market for some 8 to 9 per cent of exports and, after 1955, a source of supply of over 10 per cent of imports; indeed, in the peak year 1958 it supplied over a fifth of all imports.

The United Kingdom, the Netherlands, Switzerland and the four Scandinavian countries all recognized the Communist regime from its early days; but none of them except Britain is, or has been, an important trading partner, though there is a large Chinese diplomatic mission in Berne and Switzerland is host to the only permanent Chinese trade mission in Western Europe. Except in the case of one or two minor partners, for example Finland and Sweden, where there are bilateral government-to-government agreements renewed annually, trade results from contracts concluded between the Chinese Foreign Trade Corporations and private Western interests. It is of course subject to government control for the countries still apply the COCOM lists of strategic goods in trade with China and all exports must be licensed; moreover imports of Chinese manufactures are normally subject to quota or some other form of restriction. Although the strategic embargo is no longer sufficiently all-embracing to hamper run of the mill trade, its influence is still felt: it has, for example, prevented sales of computers to China and it can also complicate the conclusion of deals covering complete plant or vehicles. The negotiations for the sale of British aircraft, for example, ran into some initial difficulties because certain of the navigational equipment was on the embargo list. In addition, special arrangements had to be made in order not to contravene the total embargo placed by the United States on trade with China: normally, instruments for the planes were bought from a British subsidiary of an American company; because trade with China was involved a British supplier had to be used. As Chinese purchases of western machinery grow, the limitations imposed by the embargo cannot but become more evident; though there is no reason why it should be more of a restraint on trade with China than it is on trade with U.S.S.R., provided that the Chinese do not choose to make an issue of it.

The first post-Korean meeting-place of Chinese and Westerners interested in trading with each other was the Moscow International Economic Conference of April 1952, at which Chinese delegates signed unofficial agreements with representatives of Belgium, Finland, France, Western Germany, Italy, the Netherlands, Switzerland and the United Kingdom. Shortly thereafter, however, Chinese and Western traders began to visit each others' countries in search of trading opportunities; and though at first there was not much business to be done, the relaxation of the embargo stimulated interest and activity, while the eclipse of Russian influence since 1960 has set

Western (and Japanese) industrialists agog to find out what the Chinese market holds for them. There have in recent months been a number of western missions to China and western goods have been exhibited in growing volume; more visits and further exhibitions are planned. As earnest of its genuine interest in what the West has to sell, China sent its first high-level trade mission to Western Europe in the summer of 1963, under Lu Hsu-chang, vice-Minister of Foreign Trade. Mr. Lu visited Britain, Switzerland (where he also made contact with a French delegation) and the Netherlands, where he signed a contract for the purchase of an urea plant.

TRADE OF TWELVE[a] WITH CHINA

	1954	1958	1962
Exports to China			
Total, $ million	89.4	443.8	148.4
Shares, percentages	100	100	100
West Germany	24	37	21
U.K.	22	17	16
France	10[b]	9	29
Italy	7[b]	7	13
Other eight	37	30	21
Imports from China			
Total, $ million	100.5	185.6	180.5
Shares, percentages	100	100	100
West Germany	36	31	22
U.K.	25	28	36
France	9[b]	5	9
Italy	2[b]	7	8
Other eight	28	29	25

a. In addition to the four named in the table: Austria, Belgium/ Luxemburg, Denmark, Finland, Netherlands, Norway, Sweden, Switzerland.   b. May include a small amount of trade with Taiwan.

Source Appendix 3.

Other than the United Kingdom, West Germany, Italy and France, which recognized the Peking Government in January 1964, are China's important Western European trade partners; for the five years 1956-60 Belgium/Luxemburg was a significant supplier of steel and Sweden provided not inconsiderable quantities of the metal in 1958-60. But the big four are consistently responsible for the lion's share on both sides of the account.

The Four Majors

It is a moot point whether any valid conclusions can be drawn from the changing proportions of trade accounted for by the main partners. Germany's exceptionally large share of exports in 1958 was due to the fact that it captured big orders for steel plate and tube, presumably at least in part from Japan, with which China severed trade links in May; recently, however, when steel purchases were resumed on a substantial scale, Japan and the United Kingdom seem to have had the luck of the draw. France's prominent showing in exports in 1962 and 1963 was thanks to grain sales, which may never be required on the same scale in future if China succeeds in covering its needs over and above domestic production by long-term agreements with Canada, Australia and other major non-European producers. The United Kingdom emerged as the largest import market in 1962 because in that year (as in the previous three years) China sold silver on the London market for sterling with which to pay for Canadian and Australian grain. In short, it would be dangerous to discern trends where exceptional circumstances are the rule.

The chart on the opposite page shows clearly the four phases in the recent history of West Europe's exports to China: embargo, relaxation, crisis, recovery (as yet incipient). There is little doubt that the CHINCOM list exercised very considerable restraint on trade with China, but it could not prevent its growth; as time went by the number of embargoed items was reduced and the countries concerned got more adept at using the exceptions procedure to their own advantage. During this period official trade statistics probably slightly underestimate the level of exchanges, since strict controls encouraged evasion and embargoed goods found their way to China via Eastern Europe. The sharp rise in exports in the year following the easing of the embargo is proof, if such were needed, of the Soviet Bloc's inadequacies as a dominant supplier and substitute for the industrialized world; but the increase would have been less steep had the easing of restrictions not coincided with the up-spring of the Great Leap and been closely followed by the rupture of trade relations with Japan. The increase in sales was biggest in the case of iron and steel, though purchases of fertilizer, rolled copper and nickel,

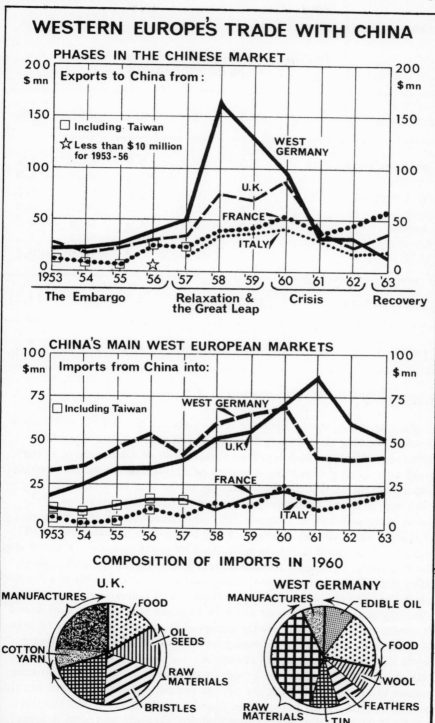

WESTERN EUROPE'S TRADE WITH CHINA

PHASES IN THE CHINESE MARKET

Exports to China from:

☐ Including Taiwan

☆ Less than $10 million for 1953-56

WEST GERMANY

U.K.

FRANCE

ITALY

The Embargo | Relaxation & the Great Leap | Crisis | Recovery

CHINA'S MAIN WEST EUROPEAN MARKETS

Imports from China into:

☐ Including Taiwan

WEST GERMANY

U.K.

FRANCE

ITALY

COMPOSITION OF IMPORTS IN 1960

U.K.

MANUFACTURES

FOOD

OIL SEEDS

COTTON YARN

RAW MATERIALS

BRISTLES

WEST GERMANY

MANUFACTURES

EDIBLE OIL

FOOD

WOOL

FEATHERS

RAW MATERIALS

TIN

machinery and synthetic fibres also rose.

IMPORTS OF IRON AND STEEL FROM
W. EUROPE AND JAPAN

$ million	1957	1958	1959	1960	1961
Belgium/Luxemburg	0.5	27.1	9.3	22.8	1.0
France	5.0	29.6	25.1	26.8	6.9
W. Germany	5.8	76.0	30.1	34.9	5.2
Italy	1.8	12.8	3.9	5.7	0.5
Austria	1.5	1.2	4.4	10.3	0.2
Sweden	0.3	6.6	5.0	3.2	1.3
U.K.	2.2	11.9	15.3	16.6	3.2
Total of above	17.2	165.2	93.1	120.3	18.3
Japan	12.1	18.3	-	-	7.4

Sources   OECD; Monthly Statistics of Japan.

This spending spree sent the trade balance, until 1955 in China's favour, soaring in Europe's favour; for it started just when the Chinese authorities had deprived themselves of all means of accurately assessing the country's export potential and it was not brought under control until after the beginning of the bad harvests. In late 1958 and 1959 the Chinese export corporations hopelessly overcommitted themselves towards European purchasers on a wide range of mainly agricultural produce on the basis of politically-inspired reports of fabulous harvests submitted by party cadres. Finding that their purchasing agents returned from the countryside with a mere tithe of the expected supplies, obligations to the Soviet Bloc were met while those to the West went by default. The behaviour of the Chinese officials at this time was so inept as to make it plain that they found themselves faced with a wholly unexpected situation; for fear of loss of face, they would give no explanation of failure to meet delivery dates (hitherto scrupulously observed) and would not admit to crop failures until long after the event; and when they finally did so they refuse to claim force majeure and so permit buyers to cancel resale contracts with small loss. This blundering lost them, for the time being, their well-deserved reputation for straight and open dealing.

The recovery in trade with Western Europe that started in 1963 is too young yet to have shown its true colours, but it is fairly clear that China has decided that its industrialization programme must now rely to a much greater extent than hitherto on Western and Japanese machinery. This implies a considerable change in the composition of Western Europe's exports to China; up to now China has not bought very substantial quantities of Western machinery, though it has been a regular buyer, mainly from Britain and Western Germany. Its principal imports from the United Kingdom have been wool, iron and steel, chemicals and non-ferrous metals; from Western Germany, chemicals and iron and steel; from France, iron and steel, fertilizers, man-made fibres and, in the last three years, cereals; and from Italy, fertilizers and man-made fibres. It is now, however, greatly widening its interests: at the end of 1963 and the beginning of 1964 contracts were signed for the delivery of no fewer than six complete plants during the next two to three years: one fertilizer factory each from the United Kingdom and the Netherlands, two fertilizer factories and a petroleum refinery from Italy, and an alcohol plant from France. Negotiations are said to be in an advanced stage for the purchase of an L/D steel smelter from Austria and a paper mill from Sweden. During his tour, Minister Lu expressed interest in mining machinery, scientific instruments, tractors, agricultural machinery, etc.; and there are a number of Chinese technical missions in Europe examining specific possibilities and obtaining know-how on, for example, the exploitation and use of natural gas at the Lacq deposits in France. This burst of activity is perhaps not quite as sudden as would appear on the surface; the first inklings of serious Chinese interest in Western capital equipment came with the $5.6 million order for Vickers Viscount aircraft placed in 1961 and the contract for Rootes' trucks signed at about the same time. And some at least of the orders for complete plant have their roots in tentative approaches begun before the crisis years.

If the character of Western Europe's sales to China is likely to change once again and to diverge still further from the prewar pattern, there remains a certain sameness about China's exports regardless of the political complexion of the formulators of economic policy. Eggs and tung oil are now of declining significance, but throughout the postwar period Chinese oilseeds and hides and skins have been fairly generally acceptable in Western Europe. Britain is still a market for tea, though fashion tends to favour the Indian variety even more than it did before the war; France has recently bought quite useful quantities. Silk continues to be imported, principally by France, Italy and Switzerland; wool (cashmere) by the United Kingdom and Italy; bristles by the United Kingdom; essential oils by France; bed-feathers and intestines by West Germany. In recent

years West Germany has also bought quite large amounts of Chinese
tin and Britain has allowed small quantities of Chinese unbleached
textile yarn to enter the country; in 1961 and 1962 the largest single
category of goods bought by Italy from China was textile fabrics and
clothing. Thus, although there is some slight evidence of diversification, the range continues to be very narrow and presents a slender
foundation on which to build a growing volume of trade.

JAPANESE SWITCHBACK

Trade and Politics

The failure of China and Japan to re-establish a satisfactory political relationship has inhibited the growth of postwar trade between
the two countries and in some years brought it to a virtual standstill.
On the face of it, Japan is the obvious source of so much that China
needs both for its industrialization and for its agriculture. It is
nearer to China than any other industrial nation; it owes much of
its cultural heritage to China; it uses a language allied to Chinese.
But Japan's postwar alignment with the United States, its cordial
relations with Taiwan, memories of its Manchurian adventure and
the Sino-Japanese war, and, perhaps, jealousy of the fact that Japan
has long since absorbed Western techniques, have all bedevilled
recent relations between the two countries. All this has contributed
to the uneven performance of Sino-Japanese trade in the past decade.
Immediately after the war the exchange of Chinese foodstuffs,
coal, iron ore and salt against Japanese machine tools, steel and
chemicals was resumed, and turnover in 1950 reached $60 million;
but the imposition of the U.N. embargo reduced the figure to $15
million in 1952. In that year came the first of a series of agreements
negotiated by the Chinese authorities and private interests in Japan
that sought to raise trade to the $100 million a year mark. The
first agreement - for $84 million each way (the amount was in fact
expressed as the round sum of £30 million) - was only 5 to 6 per
cent fulfilled; the second, for the same sum and signed in October
1953, was rather more successful, being some 40 per cent fulfilled;
the third, again for $84 million, was signed in May 1955 and having
been three-quarters carried out in sixteen months was extended to
May 1957 and somewhat enlarged. There followed nearly a year of
hard bargaining, during which trade slackened again, before a fourth
agreement was reached in March 1958.
There were a number of points at issue but the most thorny was
the status and composition of the permanent trade missions that it

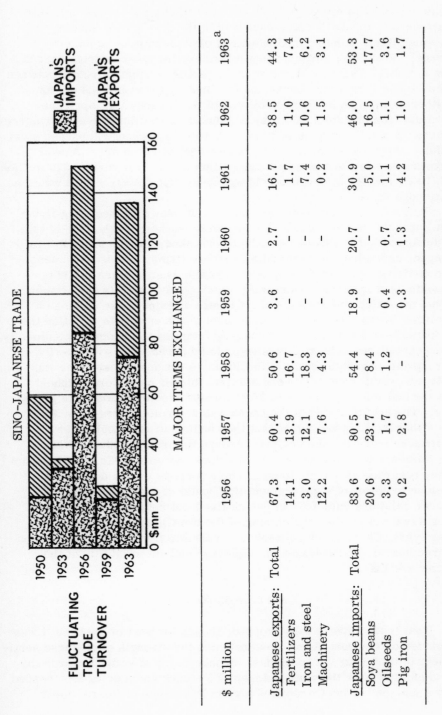

SINO-JAPANESE TRADE

FLUCTUATING TRADE TURNOVER

MAJOR ITEMS EXCHANGED

$ million	1956	1957	1958	1959	1960	1961	1962	1963[a]
Japanese exports: Total	67.3	60.4	50.6	3.6	2.7	16.7	38.5	44.3
Fertilizers	14.1	13.9	16.7	–	–	1.7	1.0	7.4
Iron and steel	3.0	12.1	18.3	–	–	7.4	10.6	6.2
Machinery	12.2	7.6	4.3	–	–	0.2	1.5	3.1
Japanese imports: Total	83.6	80.5	54.4	18.9	20.7	30.9	46.0	53.3
Soya beans	20.6	23.7	8.4	–	–	5.0	16.5	17.7
Oilseeds	3.3	1.7	1.2	0.4	0.7	1.1	1.1	3.6
Pig iron	0.2	2.8	–	0.3	1.3	4.2	1.0	1.7

a. January – September.

Source Monthly Statistics of Japan.

was proposed to exchange. When it was finally hammered out, this agreement, for $98 million each way in the next twelve months, seemed likely to mark the beginnings of a resumption of normal trade; in addition to exchanging missions, the two countries agreed to simplify **trade** procedures and to settle accounts directly between the Japanese exchange banks and the Bank of China instead of, as hitherto, through the London offices of these banks. In April the Yawata Iron and Steel Company concluded an unofficial five-year agreement, to a value of $280 million each way, to exchange Japanese steel plate, sheet and tubes against Chinese coal and iron ore. Annual exchanges were to rise from $28 million in the first year to $76 million in 1962, and Premier Chou held out hopes that the agreement would be extended for a further five years.

Neither agreement was carried out. In May a Chinese flag flying in Nagasaki was torn down by a Japanese worker; in the face of this "dishonour", the Peking Government revoked licences to trade with Japan, cancelled contracts with Japanese firms, withdrew Chinese trade delegates from Japan, sent Japanese businessmen in China packing and launched a blistering attack on Mr. Kishi's Government. This most flagrant example of a Chinese attempt to use trade as a political weapon was the culmination of years of efforts to entice the Japanese from the American camp by tempting the business community, who showed themselves all too eager to be persuaded, with glowing prospects of greater trade with China. A cat and mouse game was played: small contracts were allotted; bigger ones were withheld at the last moment; fears of West European competition were played up. The actual timing of the break was determined largely by the fact that the Chinese judged that they had a sufficient hold over Japanese industry, particularly through the iron and steel contract, to influence the coming general elections and unseat Mr. Kishi, whom they regarded as a U.S. toady. Their purpose was to ensure the return to power of a government that would recognize Peking and sever relations with Taiwan (which itself cut relations with Japan for a few weeks after the signing of the two Chinese contracts). In the event, China deprived itself of a valuable trade partner for some three years; it also learnt the weakness and unrealiability of the Japanese Left.

A Fresh Start

That trade never wholly stopped, though for part of the time it was carried on via Hong Kong, demonstrates the strength of business sentiment in its favour. The Chinese attitude began to soften towards the end of 1960 after the visit to Japan of a trades union delegation headed by a member of the Committee for the Promotion of International

Trade. Premier Chou laid down unacceptable terms, including the recognition of Peking and the severance of relations with Taiwan, for the conduct of trade on a government-to-government basis, which he said should be the normal method; but he also indicated that China would be prepared to trade through agreements with private firms friendly to China (these so-called friendly firms, designated by the Japan Socialist Party and the Sohyo Labour Federation, increased greatly in number as relations became more normal and the volume of trade expanded). On this basis, exchanges gathered momentum and the long process of normalizing relations was embarked on once again.

Though there is still no inter-governmental accord between the two countries, trade is now unofficial only in name; the mission which negotiated the present agreement was headed by Mr. Takasaki a former Minister of International Trade and Industry, and the government was consulted at all stages and approved the arrangements made. The agreement was signed late in 1962 and calls for trade of $500 million each way over the five years 1963-67 in the form of individual transactions concluded between private Japanese interests and the China National Foreign Trade Corporation. Although at first much was made of the barter element in the deal, this soon faded away to no more than an intention to maintain trade in overall balance over the five-year period. Cash settlements are in sterling or any other mutually acceptable currency and, though it was originally decided that payments should be made via London, in 1963 the Bank of Tokyo reopened its correspondent contract with the Bank of China so that the head offices of the two banks will be able to exchange letters of credit directly.

During 1963 arrangements were worked out for credit sales by Japan, both medium and longer-term. In the first flush of enthusiasm the Japanese were somewhat over-generous in their offers, partly it would appear because they suspected West European merchants of stealing a march on them. The Ministry of International Trade and Industry (MITI) felt obliged, for example, to disallow contracts for deferred payments that made no provision for an initial down-payment. It also intervened in the protracted negotiations that led up to the first contract for the sale of a complete plant by Japan to China. Initially Kurashiki Rayon proposed to sell the Chinese a vinylon plant at a price of $20.6 million on terms of 25 per cent down payment and the balance over five years. Interest was set at 4.5 per cent, a figure above which the Chinese are reluctant to go. On MITI's insistence the interest charge was raised to 6 per cent and the price lowered to $20 million. On smaller deals, many of which are currently under consideration, the terms normally asked are 20 per cent cash down, and the balance over eighteen months to three years, at 5 per

cent interest. In a recent instance the extension of the repayment
period to four years resulted in the quick conclusion of a contract to
supply 61,560 tons of ordinary steel to a value of $11.35 million.

By the end of 1963 trade between the two countries was probably
running not far short of the target figure, though for the year as a
whole it was $137 million - slightly below the postwar peak of $151
million in 1956. To compensate for this the programme fixed up
at the end of 1963 for the current year provides for a total of $122
million each way. The main items being exchanged are, as always,
Chinese soya beans, industrial salt, coking coal and iron ore against
Japanese steel, fertilizers and machinery. It looks at last as though
all were set for the smooth development of trade, yet there is little
or no talk of attempting to exceed the amounts set in the agreement,
despite the fact that they were so easily reached. The lack of Chinese
export goods is still a severe limitation on trade growth; there have
been many complaints since trade was resumed in 1961 about the quality of Chinese deliveries and about the prices of, for example, coal.
In the case of iron ore, Japan has sought out alternative supplies
during the last few years and fixed up long-term contracts that will
satisfy its needs, often up to 1966 or 1967, with a much higher-grade
material than China can provide. Businessmen, already badly hit by
the abrupt halting of trade in 1958, have no wish to become unduly
dependent on a trade partner that mixes politics with business, nor
are they or the Japanese Government prepared to endanger textile
markets in the United States or fertilizer markets in Taiwan by playing along too closely with Peking.

Sales of complete plant, however, fall outside the scope of the
agreement and it is here that trade may expand; at the time of writing,
it was reported that the contract for a second vinylon plant had been
finalized and a third was under negotiation. If the non-Communist
world is to fill the gap left by the withdrawal of the Soviet Union and
its European allies, Japan cannot afford to be left behind. And it has
so many natural advantages over its West European competitors.

ASIAN SURPLUSES

Hong Kong - and Macao

Hong Kong's importance as a trans-shipment centre for Chinese
trade was at its height in the first three years of the Communist regime;
this business was dealt a resounding blow by the imposition of the
embargo and has since shown a downwards trend broken only in 1958
after the severance of direct trade links between China and Japan, when

the Japanese Trade Ministry sanctioned limited transactions via the colony. Hong Kong's present significance for China is as a source of foreign exchange, arising both from the huge trade deficit and from the remittances of Overseas Chinese. In addition it provides a meeting place for Chinese and foreigners, where talks and negotiations can be held in a more relaxed atmosphere than could be found behind the Bamboo Curtain. There are less tangible advantages, too, for a country as isolated as China in having an ear on the world.

HONG KONG'S TRADE WITH CHINA

$ million	Hong Kong's Exports		Hong Kong's Imports	Balance to Hong Kong
	Total	of which Re-exports		
1951	305	...	162	+143
1952	91	...	145	- 54
1957	22	...	198	-176
1958	27	...	245	-218
1959	20	19	181	-161
1960	21	19	208	-187
1961	17	16	180	-163
1962	15	14	212	-197
1963	12	11	260	-248

... Not available.

Source Hong Kong Trade Statistics.

The largest items re-exported in recent years have been non-ferrous base metals, fertilizers and chemicals, but small quantities of an enormous variety of goods pass into China via the colony. Hong Kong's own exports to China are negligible in size but can be important at times of sudden shortages of certain commodities; for example early in 1964 the Colony proved a handy source of plastic raw materials badly needed by Chinese factories that were being urged to raise supplies of plastic household goods to the domestic market. On the other hand, Hong Kong takes an average of about a fifth of all its imports from China. Food and textiles (excluding clothing) are by far the largest purchases; the quality of food supplies, particularly of fruit and vegetables, was greatly improved by the opening in 1962 of an express freight service from Wuhan to Canton, which cut the journey from eight days to fifty-two hours.

China's trade relations with Macao are a miniature of those with Hong Kong: the Portuguese colony, too, yields a satisfactory surplus both on the trade and the remittance accounts. Imports from China in 1962 were worth $12.6 million and exports less than $300,000; to this can be added remittances estimated at $10 million and postal goods valued at some $4 million - mainly Chinese food re-exported (against payment of duties) to indigent relatives in Kwantung.

West to Pakistan

Leaving aside Japan, where comparison must be with Western Europe, no other Asian country approaches Hong Kong in importance to China - the colony alone regularly takes more than half of all China's exports to Asia - but there are other useful surpluses to be earned from other Asian members of the Sterling Area and vital raw materials to be bought. Malaya and Singapore with their large Chinese populations are a regular market for Chinese goods and are normally a target of Chinese export drives. In the early 'fifties, purchases from China averaged $30 million to $40 million a year while sales there never reached even $10 million; but in 1957 with the lifting of the embargo China began to buy Malayan rubber in quantity and to step up its exports. Welcome as the first move might be, the second took little account of the normal sensitivity of a developing country to foreign goods that compete with its infant industries; the result was that in 1958 restrictions were clapped on imports from China, the Bank of China was forced to close its office in Malaya, trade began to decline again and, partly in retaliation, but more importantly because of the need to conserve sterling to pay for imports of food from Canada and Australia, China withdrew from the Malayan rubber market.

It would obviously be intolerable for Malaysia to continue running annual deficits of the order of $50 million to $60 million (the inclusion of Sabah and Sarawak's trade would tip the scales a little further in the same direction). But given somewhat more of the do-as-you-would-be-done-by spirit on China's part, there is a good basis for trade between the two countries to the benefit of both. China must continue to buy rubber and Chinese goods can find a market, particularly in Singapore. Apart from traditional foodstuffs, the main Chinese exports are cement (rather sporadically), textiles and clothing, which are highly competitive with all-comers price-wise if not always quality-wise, and such things as tyres, which became very popular during 1962 and earned an excellent reputation for durability but were hit by the imposition of a 70 per cent duty in early 1963.

PAN-MALAYAN TRADE WITH CHINA

$ million	Imports from China			Exports to China		Balance to Malaya
	Total	of which Food	Manu- factures	Total	of which Rubber	
1957	52.2	26.9	16.9	24.2	19.4	-28.0
1958	63.9	29.6	25.4	38.0	34.9	-25.9
1959	51.1	19.8	33.1	39.7	37.5	-11.4
1960	57.1	23.3	23.8	28.4	24.0	-28.7
1961	56.3	24.9	23.0	3.8	1.6	-52.5
1962	65.9	28.3	29.0	0.8	0.4	-65.1

Source   Malayan External Trade Statistics.

Surpluses are also usually earned by China in trade with Burma and Indonesia but these must be in part at least financed by Chinese aid (see next Chapter), which is not extended to Malaya, and they are in any case of limited value since they are non-transferable. Burma is a useful source of rice to China; as early as 1954 an agreement was signed for the exchange of 150,000 to 200,000 tons of Burmese rice a year against Chinese industrial equipment over the years 1955-57, and Burmese rice is used in meeting most of China's commitments under the rice/rubber pacts with Ceylon (see below). Trade with Indonesia began to expand in 1956 but Chinese purchases did not reach significant proportions until 1957 when the embargo on rubber exports was lifted. Trade then increased substantially, financed in part by China itself.

It is Ceylon, however, that is the mainstay of China's rubber supplies. The island, not then a member of the United Nations, felt no obligation to apply the embargo on trade in strategic goods with China, and in 1952 concluded a five-year agreement for the annual exchange of 270,000 tons of Chinese rice against 50,000 tons of sheet rubber. At this period China had no alternative source of supply and agreed to pay a price well above the world price; but when the agreement expired at the end of 1957 the Peking Govern- ment was in a stronger bargaining position and took the opportunity both to reduce its dependence on Ceylonese supplies and to cut the premium which it paid. The third rice/rubber pact, now in force, covers 1963-67 and provides for the annual exchange of approximately 200,000 tons of rice against 30,000 tons of rubber (though in 1963, 33,000 tons was to be shipped). The price now paid is that ruling

in Singapore or a few cents higher. Apart from rice, Ceylon buys
small quantities of Chinese textiles, mainly dyed and printed cotton
piecegoods; but on the whole trade is on a rather lower plane than
it was ten years ago. Though China has at times been in debt over
its exchanges with the island, trade is now approximately in balance.
The apparent Chinese deficit shown in Ceylon's trade returns is
accounted for by the fact that imports are attributed to the country
of origin, so that Burmese rice paid for by China counts as an import
from Burma not from China.

Even before the frontier dispute flared up, China's trade with
India was no better than desultory (apart from the regular trickle of
goods in transit for Tibet) and for the present there do not seem
many grounds for supposing that it will prosper. India has few raw
materials surplus to its own needs and required by China; it would
certainly not welcome Chinese light industrial products in its home
market or tolerate the building up of Chinese trade surpluses.
Prospects for trade with Pakistan are perhaps rather better, and
the 1964 visit of Premier Chou and Foreign Minister Cheng Yi may
help to enliven exchanges. Until early 1963 trade was governed by
barter arrangements in respect of individual commodities; in
January 1963, however, a formal trade agreement, embodying a
most-favoured-nation clause, was signed; valid for one year in
the first instance, it is renewed automatically unless either side
wishes to terminate. China is to export metals (including steel),
coal, cement, machinery, chemicals and cereals against cotton,
jute and manufactures, leather, textiles, chrome ore and newsprint. In the first eight months of 1963 Chinese purchases from
Pakistan did, in fact, rise substantially, to $9 million from less
than $2 million in the same months of 1962, but Pakistan took only
$3.5 million worth of Chinese goods compared with $2.8 million
in January-August 1962.

And Beyond

To date, China's trade with the Asian Middle East has been
very small beer indeed, but it has not passed entirely unnoticed -
certainly not by Japan which, on the whole, has been more vociferous
in complaining of Chinese competition in this area than in South
East Asia. Since 1959 China has had a useful market in Iraq and
in 1962, the latest year for which figures are available, exports
were little short of $10 million. The agreement for 1963 foresaw
further expansion with China supplying industrial equipment, elec-
trical appliances, and textiles, and taking in exchange petroleum
and products, dates and wool. With Syria, too, the 'sixties have
brought a great improvement in the level of trade, which should be

further enhanced by the agreements on trade, payments and economic and technical cooperation signed early in 1963. In January–September that year, Syrian exports to China, mainly of cotton, reached $16 million against under $4 million a year earlier, while imports from China in both years were rather over $4 million.

CANADA AND AUSTRALIA

Although in the past three years China has shopped for food in every continent, it has made its major purchases in Canada and Australia. Trade with these countries rocketed to prominence in 1961 when China's imports entered the $100 million category; they had never previously reached even $10 million in the case of Canada, though wool buying had lifted imports from Australia to $30 million in 1959.

CANADIAN AND AUSTRALIAN TRADE
WITH CHINA

$ million	1959	1960	1961	1962	1963
Canada's					
Exports	1.8	8.7	122.8	137.0	96.9
Imports	5.2	5.6	3.2	4.3	4.6
Balance	- 3.4	+ 3.1	+119.6	+132.7	+ 92.3
Australia's					
Exports	30.1	24.0	160.8	98.6	209.7
Imports	8.4	10.8	7.2	10.7	15.2
Balance	+21.7	+13.2	+153.6	+ 87.9	+194.5

Source   Canadian and Australian Trade Statistics.

That China should import foodgrains was nothing new, for it had often in the past bought small amounts of Canadian and Australian wheat against sterling; but the agricultural disasters of 1959, 1960 and 1961 forced a change in the scale and method of buying. Even so, imports were not large in relation to domestic rice production of the order of 80 million tons a year and wheat production of 25 million tons;

wheat imports from all sources, the major item, reached 5 million
tons in 1962-63 and may be some 4 million tons in the current season.
(In this as in so many other spheres China has been outdone by the
U.S.S.R., whose current season's wheat purchases could reach 14
million tons). In all probability, the imported wheat is used mainly
to supply the central and northern seaboard cities in order to relieve
the strain on the internal transport system; it does not necessarily
imply a shift, whether forced or voluntary, from rice to wheat
consumption. China has continued to export small quantities of rice
throughout the bad times, largely it would seem for the publicity
that such deals attract and because rice commands a far higher
price than wheat; its commitment to Ceylon it has met in recent
years almost wholly with Burmese rice.

At the start of 1961 China placed orders for wheat, barley and
flour with Canada and Australia, each worth nearly $60 million; but
it must soon have become apparent that another bad harvest would
necessitate imports well beyond the country's ability to pay cash
down. In April 1961 an agreement was signed in Hong Kong whereby
Canada undertook to supply 223 million bushels of wheat, flour and
barley over the following two and a half years against 25 per cent
down payment in sterling on each shipment and the remainder in
nine months. The terms were not generous compared with those
accorded by Canada to European Communists nor with those granted
by Australia to China in 1961 on a $45 million wheat deal: 10 per
cent down, 40 per cent in six months and the remainder in twelve
months. As time passed and the Chinese established their credit-
worthiness by meeting their obligations punctually or ahead of
schedule, they were able to extract some concessions. The
seventh contract under the first Canadian agreement (signed in
December 1962) allowed twelve months to settle the balance and
the new agreement signed in 1963 extended the period to eighteen
months. Australia, too, modified its terms to 20 per cent of the
balance (after the 10 per cent down payment) in six months, 20
per cent in nine months and the rest in twelve. More recently
it appears to be allowing credit beyond a year.

There is no prospect for the present of China withdrawing
from the world grain market; it has contracted to buy at least
112 million bushels of wheat, and perhaps up to 187 million, from
Canada by mid-1966, at a total cost of about $240 million (the first
agreement was worth some $360 million). It has an agreement
with France; late in 1963 it arranged to take 1.75 million tons of
Argentinian grain by the end of 1965; and it is still in the
Australian market. But the huge imbalance in trade with the
major food suppliers is bound to be extremely embarrassing to
the Peking Government, and will become more so if it persists

after China has to start repayment of the credits just granted by Western European countries and Japan on sales of complete plant.

Both Canada and Australia have reaped immense benefit from their grain sales to China, which came at a time when bumper crops threatened to raise existing inventories to mountainous proportions. Both would like to do even more trade with China, but both tend to look upon the country as a potential market only, shelving the thornier question of how exports are to be paid for. Australian wool men forecast that by 1970 China will need 400 million to 450 million lb clean weight of wool-type fibres a year, of which 100 million lb will have to be imported at a cost, in present prices, of some $50 million to $80 million; Canadian businessmen dream of selling copper, nickel, mining and drilling equipment and general machinery to the Peking Government. Canadian textile interests, however, were less pleased when, under the current wheat contract, the Canadian Government agreed to take $7 million worth a year of "sensitive" goods from China (instead of about $1.3 million worth in 1962), mainly cotton textiles and piecegoods, shoes, toys, table lamps, and sewing machines. Although a maximum has been set for each category of goods (for example, the quota for handkerchiefs is 450,000 dozen against 3,200 dozen imported in 1962) it is claimed that this generosity will put 1,500 Canadian jobs in jeopardy. The action also raised a protest from the Japanese, who operate a voluntary quota system on sales to Canada. Nor are the Japanese pleased by another Canadian concession to Chinese protests about the definition of "fair market value" used when assessing Chinese goods for duty. Until the 1963 agreement Chinese goods were valued at prices similar to those of goods made in the United States and Britain, because these countries were taken as major suppliers. Japanese and Hong Kong goods were valued at much lower prices.

AFRICA AND LATIN AMERICA

Wooing the Newly Independent Africans

There remain Africa and Latin America, and in neither has China yet made much headway. Although there are Overseas Chinese in Madagascar, along the Pacific coast of South America, and in Cuba, contacts between China and the two continents were minimal before the war and no great effort was devoted to strengthening relations until the second half of the 'fifties. In many ways Latin America is probably more fertile ground for Chinese propaganda and influence (more capital can, for instance, be made out of anti-Americanism), but it is Africa that has so far received most attention and has been visited by senior members of the Peking Government. Fifteen African states at present recognize Communist China and many of the nineteen (largely ex-French colonies) which have diplomatic relations with Taiwan may follow General de Gaulle's lead in recognizing the Communist regime; on the American continent only Cuba has diplomatic relations with Peking.

In the winter of 1963-64, Premier Chou En-lai, accompanied by Foreign Minister Chen Yi (lately returned from Kenya's independence celebrations) and a staff of eighty, toured extensively in North and West Africa making known the Chinese presence; only the army mutinies there prevented a visit to East Africa too. The purposes of the trip were to gain firsthand information of African conditions; to disseminate knowledge of China's achievements; to sound the possibilities of calling another Afro-Asian conference similar to that held in Bandung in 1955; to discourage ideas of another Belgrade - type conference and, if possible, to poison the Nasser-Tito-Nehru friendship. In the short term, the tour brought no spectacular rewards, no devastating setbacks. African countries remained cool towards the prospect of involvement in the Sino-Soviet dispute and somewhat out of sympathy with the Chinese doctrine of self-reliance, preferring to accept aid from all sources without promising allegiance to one side or the other.

The Ministers and their entourage were not in Africa to talk trade but they may have laid the foundations for some exchanges that will be worked out in detail later by members of the Foreign Trade Corporations. Saharan oil was certainly discussed while the mission was in Algeria, and in Morocco the Premier is reported to have sounded out the possibility of extending the old triangular arrangement whereby the proceeds of Chinese sales of green tea to Morocco were used to buy badly needed machinery and equipment from France. Until 1958 Morocco had a big deficit on trade with China and even after shipments of phosphates started there was still a surplus in China's favour. The present idea is apparently to increase this surplus by greater sales of Chinese textiles and consumer goods, the resulting balance being used to buy French goods. The Chinese are evidently casting round for some means of making as good use of the Franc Zone as they do of the Sterling Area by earning in one country so that they may buy in another, and usually more industrialized, one. It is said that they have even gone so far as to suggest that France should extend credits to its ex-colonies in Africa to enable them to purchase Chinese goods, the Chinese using the francs thus earned to buy French machinery.

There is nothing in the record of China's past trade with Africa

to justify so elaborate a venture as Chou's tour. China's first real
contact with African states after the war came in 1955 at the Bandung
Conference. A trade agreement was signed with Egypt in October of
that year and an Ambassador was appointed to Cairo in 1956, whose
duties included making contact with African states south of the Sahara.
From the purely commercial point of view, Egypt's attraction for
China lay in its cotton. Under the 1955 agreement, Egypt pledged
itself to exchange $28 million worth of cotton a year for three years
against Chinese machine tools, machinery, steel, textile machinery,
a sugar refinery and certain other complete plants as well as traditional Chinese exports. Although China may at the time have had a
temporary surplus of steel, some at least of the capital goods were
re-exports of East European origin. The following year it was
planned to raise the value of exchanges by 20 per cent and by 1959,
when another three-year agreement was signed, turnover equal to
$85 million was planned. This level was again written into the 1962
three-year agreement, which provided for the exchange of Chinese
tea, frozen meat, pig iron, chemicals, dyes, paper and newsprint
(a considerably less ambitious list than that of 1955) against
Egyptian cotton, textiles and peanuts. The planned level of trade
has never been achieved and until 1961 China was always heavily in
debt to Egypt. In 1962 trade was in balance but in early 1963 Egypt's
surplus mounted again. Settlements between the two countries are
in sterling and the prices of all goods exchanged are quoted in
sterling.

Other cotton suppliers are the Sudan, Tanganyika and Uganda.
Although Chinese imports from the Sudan reached as much as $9
million in some years, a formal trade agreement between the two
countries was not signed until 1962. This embodied the principle
of most-favoured-nation treatment and also that of bringing trade
into balance; in this instance, too, China is normally the debtor.
With the other two countries there are as yet no formal agreements,
but in 1963 China bought 75,000 bales of Ugandan cotton, about one
fifth of the total crop, and this year it is expected to take 100,000
bales, making it the country's biggest customer. From Tanganyika
purchases are on a much smaller scale. China is hoping eventually
to be able to balance its buying from this area with sales of textiles
and light machinery.

For the rest in North and East Africa: a trade agreement was
signed at the end of 1963 and Somalia. It is hard to believe that
this is more than a formality designed to flatter the Somali Government, though detailed lists of goods to be exchanged have been drawn
up, including on the Chinese side textiles, metal products, machinery,
chemicals and tea, and on the Somali side oilseeds, cereals, frankin-
cense, myrrh, gum arabic, skins and minerals. This trade should

yield a surplus for China, though perhaps not a very useful one.

While China may feel more natural sympathy towards the newly independent countries of West Africa, particularly the Ghana-Guinea - Mali trio, trade with the area remains very small (and badly documented). In early 1961 a delegation from the China Africa People's Friendship Association (set up early in 1960), led by its President Liu Chang-sheng, visited the three countries and both Nkrumah and Sekou Touré have been in Peking. During Nkrumah's visit in 1961 a trade and payments agreement was signed that fixed the level of annual exchanges at $11.2 million each way; China was to export machinery, textiles, light industrial and consumer goods in exchange for cocoa and products, cotton, hides and skins, palm kernels, copra, coconut oil, tobacco, sugar, coffee and industrial diamonds. In practice, if Ghana's trade statistics (which oddly enough do not distinguish trade between the two Chinas) are to be believed, trade has never approached even half this level and there is no good reason why it should do so in future. The 1960 agreement with Guinea envisaged annual exchanges equal to $9.5 million (Chinese rice, textiles, machinery, chemicals, educational and cultural supplies against coffee, rubber, industrial diamonds, and the usual palm products); but it would be surprising indeed if figures of this magnitude were realized. Under the 1961 treaty with Mali, China again promised machinery and industrial equipment in exchange for the usual run of tropical products.

China's remaining trade partners of any importance in Africa were chosen on purely economic grounds, regardless of their ideological complexion: both the Republic of South Africa and Southern Rhodesia have supplied useful quantities of maize during the recent crisis years. China has thrice affirmed its intention of discontinuing trade with South Africa but it was still buying from there in 1963, though some deals at least were concluded through the intermediary of a French firm. The continuance of this trade has not furthered the Chinese cause in newly-liberated Africa.

Latin America - Ultima Thule

If annual trade turnover with Africa has probably exceeded $100 million only once (in 1960) in the last decade, that with Latin America seems rarely to have touched $10 million until China entered the Cuban sugar market in 1961 and the Argentinian grain market in 1962. In the early part of the 'fifties, contact between the two areas was made largely by the Communist parties of Latin America, some of whom saw in China's land reform and agricultural policy a model for their own. Since the later 'fifties, however, there has been a substantial flow of visitors in both directions, including Joao Goulart of Brazil,

who visited Peking when he was vice-President to Senor Quadros. In
1960 the China-Latin American Friendship Association was set up
under Chu Tu-nan and branches were opened in many capitals;
propaganda in Spanish and Portuguese is disseminated by periodicals
and broadcasts from Peking.

In one such broadcast, in October 1960, it was said that China
wanted Latin America's 'rich industrial raw materials and mineral
products', particularly wool from Argentina and Uruguay, nitrate
and copper from Chile, sugar from Cuba, salt from Brazil, petroleum
from Venezuela, and non-ferrous metals from many countries. In
exchange China would send tea, resin, medicinal herbs, animal products, textiles, medical and radio equipment, laboratory instruments.
"Their high quality" it was said "has won them a very good reputation."
These brave words presaged little; up-to-date data are particularly
hard to come by in this area, but it is fairly clear that trade has not
expanded markedly except with Cuba. In 1961 a trade treaty was
signed with Brazil and President Quadros agreed to the establishment
of a permanent Chinese trade mission in Rio; it was intended that
Chinese paper and chemicals should be exchanged against Brazilian
cloth, wood and tobacco to a value of $50 million, a figure that on
present showing it will take many years to approach. Prospects for
an increase in trade with Argentina are better; in 1962 the country
sold 100,000 tons of maize to China and at the end of 1963 a contract
was signed under which, before the end of 1965, 1.75 million tons of
Argentinian grain (including wheat, maize, oats, sorghum and linseed)
will be delivered to China against payment in sterling.

Wool has been bought from Uruguay in small quantities, and at the
end of 1963 Chile decided to sell 10,000 tons of copper to China to a
value of $8 million, payable in hard currency. This last phrase perhaps
gives the clue to why China has not bothered to cultivate trade relations with Latin America. Chinese produce is not required in the area
and could not surmount the high protective tariff walls with which the
Latin Americans surround themselves; there is no chance of covering
imports by exports, let alone of building up a surplus for use in other
areas; and even if a surplus were earned, the problem of transferring
it would probably be insuperable. For most things that Latin America
produces there are alternative sources of supply which represent a
softer option as far as payment is concerned.

In the case of Cuba the matter is different; China is vying with the
Soviet Union and bidding for another disciple, while Cuba itself is not
above playing the rivals off against each other: veering to China's view
on the test ban treaty yet at the same time committing itself to large
deliveries of sugar to the U.S.S.R. in 1965-70 against payment in
Soviet goods. This latest agreement with the Russians would indeed
seem to be something of a check for the Chinese; they are certainly

in no position to go one better. By their agreement of August 1960 they were assured of 2.5 million long tons of Cuban sugar over five years; that means that deliveries will finish this year and unless Cuban production rises very fast it seems doubtful whether there will be much surplus over and above Russian requirements. In addition to sugar, China buys Cuban nickel, copper, manganese, chrome and cobalt, tobacco, beans and cowhides. In the first year 20 per cent of the sugar was paid for in sterling; but for the rest exchanges are supposed to be on a barter basis, with the Chinese sending in both 1962 and 1963 rice, rolled steel, machinery, chemicals, medical equipment, among other things. The agreement for 1964 promises Cuba heavy steel sheet and other heavy equipment, chemical products, drugs, cotton cloth, tinned meat and, again, rice.

5

A MODEST PROGRAMME

The extension of foreign aid by China was an integral part of planning from the start of the first Five-Year Plan. At the beginning, assistance was given only to Communist countries which were, with the exception of Albania, Asian neighbours. But in 1956 first Cambodia, then Nepal, Indonesia, and, after the Suez crisis, Egypt, all became recipients of Chinese help. Thereafter the flow broadened: not much aid was given in 1957, but Ceylon received a loan; in 1958 there was renewed activity, with Burma and Yemen among the newcomers; and in 1959 help to an undisclosed amount was given to the Algerian rebels. In 1960 the first aid agreement with Africa south of the Sahara was signed; this provided help for Guinea's three-year plan. In 1961 aid was also extended to Ghana and Mali and to Cuba. It seems doubtful whether any new aid was granted in 1962, but in 1963 the flow began again and Syria, Somalia and Algeria were added to the list; in February 1964 Zanzibar was accorded a small sum of money in token of more to come and presented with a few Chinese tractors gratis.

It is difficult to assess the total value of aid so far given by China partly because in the earlier years sums were quoted in yuan, partly because it is sometimes difficult to judge whether a particular agreement is a new one or whether it merely implements promises made earlier, partly because some of the projects under aid agreements are hardly begun within the specified period let alone completed. Appendix 5 summarizes the agreements known to have been made with various countries between 1953 and the early weeks of 1964; it does not claim completeness and unfortunately, for lack of information, leaves interesting aspects of individual loans unclear. Ignoring the sums quoted only in yuan (given to Mongolia, North Korea and North Vietnam in 1953 and 1955), China would appear (in round figures) to have committed itself to the following aid in terms of dollar equivalent up to the end of 1963. To convert the sums to dollars is not to imply that Chinese aid is the equivalent of the same value of aid given by the U.S. Most Chinese aid is tied to Chinese goods and nothing is known about the method of calculating the prices

of aid deliveries. More than half the exceptionally large figure for
1961 is accounted for by long-term loans to Albania and North Vietnam.

CHINESE AID

$ million			
1954	15$_a$	1960	265
1955	–	1961	430
1956	100	1962	–
1957	65	1963	90
1958	120		
1959	45	Total	1,130

a. Only aid quoted in yuan was given in this year.

Source   Appendix 5.

   There has been some surprise that China should be able to help
others while its own circumstances remain so straitened. But it is
hardly a matter of choice: so long as it is vying for world leadership,
China cannot opt out of the struggle to make friends and influence
people by offering assistance towards speedy development. The
Chinese Government is confident that in the long run three factors
will play into its hands and make Chinese aid far and away more
acceptable than that of the West or the Soviet Union. In the first
place, the Chinese are non-European and non-white. So far this has
proved a difficult card to play for the Chinese attitude that all foreigners are barbarians is not to be changed overnight; African students
have found Peking as unfriendly a place to live as Moscow. Abroad
Chinese experts and technicians are no better at mixing freely and
unobtrusively with the local population than are their Soviet confreres;
and the fact that they are paid the same as a local would be paid for
doing the same job, and therefore enjoy no higher a standard of living,
tends to lower China's prestige and underline its poverty rather than
to create the desired image of Big Brother too putting his shoulder to
the wheel. Secondly, the Chinese claim to be the only aid-giving
country with a genuinely underdeveloped economy, the only one, therefore, in a position to understand the problems of industrialization and
to provide the advice and the means to solve them at least cost. This,
potentially, is a bull point, for if China could devise simple forms of
farm mechanization and electrification and a solution to the problem

of finding productive work for the displaced rural population, it would be a boon to countries such as India, Indonesia or Pakistan. However, for the present China is in no position to boast of its agricultural prowess. Lastly, the Chinese claim - and with some justification - that they, too, have suffered colonialism, and are still victims of imperialism.

MOTIVES AND MANIFESTATIONS

Aid to Communist Countries

If in the long run aid-giving is one aspect of the struggle for world leadership, in the short run it has a great many functions to fulfil that are perhaps best illustrated in relation to individual cases rather than by generalization. In the case of Communist countries, China's first aim is to hold its own vis-a-vis the Soviet Union; Albania must be maintained as a bridgehead in Europe, whence Chinese broadsides can be fired into the heart of Eastern Europe. So important is it that it is one of the few countries on whose behalf China is willing to part with foreign exchange so that machinery not made in Chinese factories can be bought in Western Europe. Albania was first reported to have received Chinese aid in 1953, but no details were furnished; in 1954 it got a small grant and a loan - in total equal to some $15 million - to be used over the period 1955-60. This was followed in 1959 by a further credit of $13.75 million to be used during 1961-65 to buy various types of machinery, including that for a cotton mill, a flax mill and a glassworks. Some of the money appears to have been used to buy Italian equipment, for Albanian purchases from Italy rose in 1961.

The Chinese made their really big gesture in 1961 when they lent Albania the equivalent of $125 million to buy machinery for twenty-five industrial plants; protocols for the implementation of the agreement were signed in 1962 and again in 1963. Another gesture, far less costly to China though more newsworthy since it came at the height of the Chinese food shortages, was to ship Canadian wheat to Albania. The quantities were significant in relation to the total consumption of 1.7 million Albanians, if not to that of some 700 million Chinese.

Hungary is the only other East European to have been given Chinese aid. In 1956 it received a gift equal to $7.5 million to help with reconstruction and this was followed in May 1957 by a loan of $30 million at 2 per cent per annum, to be repaid in machinery in 1960-69 - a possible explanation for Hungary's continued shipments of complete plant to China. Half the loan was in foreign currency.

Since that date no further loans have been made to Russia's European allies.

China cannot be considered particularly lucky in its Asian Communist neighbours; North Vietnam, for example, is regarded by another Communist state - East Germany - as a bottomless pit into which it is useless to pour aid in the form either of money or equipment. China cannot, however, shrug off the problem as lightly. Its first exercise in neighbourly economic aid appears to have made a virtue of necessity: in 1953 trade debts accumulated by Mongolia and North Korea were cancelled. At the same time North Korea got a grant of 800 million yuan to be spread over the years 1954-57, of which 300 million is said to have been used in 1954. In 1958 the country, which was an ardent supporter of the Great Leap philosophy, received an interest-free loan of $10 million to build a hydro-electric power station and another of $42.5 million at 1 per cent interest a year to build a textile mill and two paper mills. This was followed in 1960 by a credit of some $105 million to finance the building in 1961-64 of a range of factories for which China is supplying plant and technical expertise.

Mongolia had to wait until 1956 for further help; it then received a grant equal to $40 million to finance trade in 1956-59. In 1958 it received a loan of $25 million at 2.5 per cent per annum to buy equipment for textile mills and power plants in 1959-61. Despite this it continued to run up trade debts, which were again cancelled in 1960.

The first help to North Vietnam about which much can be established was the 800 million yuan grant of 1955 to finance railway construction in 1955-59; this might well be classed as Chinese strategic expenditure rather than aid. It was followed in 1959 by a grant of 100 million yuan and a loan of 300 million yuan at 1 per cent per annum interest, repayable in goods over 10 years starting in 1967; both of these were to finance industrial construction.

The only other Communist country to have benefited from China's generosity is Cuba and here the motive for aid was two-fold: to establish a bridgehead in Latin America, and to turn the tables on the Russians by using anti-Americanism as a weapon against them. The first loan came in 1960 when Cuba was given $60 million, interest-free, to buy complete sets of equipment for twenty-four plants over the years 1961-65. Then in May 1963 China announced a long-term interest-free loan to the amount of its surplus on trade with Cuba in 1962 and 1963 - an unknown quantity and a somewhat puzzling one, since it would not have been surprising had there been a Chinese deficit on trade in these years. This may be an example of China making a graceful gesture in circumstances where more concrete action would be wasted. It will be interesting to see whether a meaningful new aid agreement is drawn up next year.

A Helping Hand in Asia

China's motives in helping the uncommitted countries are less
directly anti-Russian and more directly anti-imperialist. Getting
to know the strengths and weaknesses of neighbours is an important
consideration in the case of Burma, Nepal, Laos, and Cambodia;
making friends with suppliers of vital raw materials in the case of
Ceylon and Indonesia; while, inevitably, the establishment and maintenance of bridgeheads plays an important part in Africa and the
Middle East. Most of the countries selected for aid are very small;
of the thirteen uncommitted nations that have received help since
1956, only three - Indonesia, Egypt and Burma - have populations
exceeding 11 million. Careful dispensation of even very small sums
can make a good showing in such circumstances. But the results
achieved have not always been as gratifying as the Chinese might
have wished. Ceylon and Nepal, for example, have been tardy in
making use of proffered help. The 1957 and 1958 agreements with
Ceylon, which should have expired in 1962, were both extended at
Ceylon's request, one for five years the other for three, because
credits involved had not been fully used owing to the inability of the
Ceylonese Government to execute its own ambitious development
plans. In Nepal likewise, Chinese plans to build a paper mill and
cement plant foundered partly because initial assessment of the raw
material base and the means of overcoming transport difficulties
was over-optimistic, partly no doubt on Nepalese lethargy - which
has delayed work on the Nepal stretch of the Kathmandu-Lhasa road,
financed by China. A small Chinese-built tannery is, however,
nearing completion and the feasibility of other projects is under
study.
The Yemen has been another slow starter; the Hodeida-Sanaa road
project has been opened with a fanfare of trumpets, but not even
Chinese energy has been enough to set the country on the road to
industrialization. The aid agreement signed in 1958 went into eclipse
during the Yemen's political upheavals but was revived and extended
in late 1962. The reasons for the initial agreement remain obscure,
for it was made with what was probably the world's most reactionary
and despotic government; it could have been a preliminary move in a
plan to discomfort Britain in Aden, or it might have been aimed
ultimately at Saudi Arabia and its oil.
The loan given to Cambodia in 1956 proved insufficient to complete
the textile, plywood, cement, and paper factories planned and was supplemented by a further grant in 1961. At least one of the plants so far
completed - the cement factory - is not a great success and Prince
Sihanouk has ruefully admitted that it costs a good deal more to
make cement locally than to import it. Possibly the Chinese

geologists who spent three years surveying the country gave undue
weight to political considerations and once again assessed the raw
material base through rosy spectacles. Be that as it may discussions
are under way about the setting up of a Chinese-financed cotton
spinnery and a glass factory, the geologists having apparently
established the existence of deposits of high-grade glass sand.

In both Laos and Burma the Chinese are helping in road construction, in particular in strengthening links with Southern China.
Burma was lent the equivalent of some $4 million in 1958 at 2.5
per cent a year to build a cotton spinning mill; the factory came
into operation within eighteen months and is reported to compare
favourably with a similar plant financed by U.S. aid. But the big
loan, this time free of interest, did not materialize until 1961; it
is worth $84 million and is being used to buy complete plant and
technical aid during 1961-67. Repayment does not start until 1971.
The Economic and Technical Cooperation Agreement that enshrined
this loan enabled China to send some hundred experts to Burma in
March 1962, most of whom stayed for more than a year and some
of whom are still there. In the autumn of 1962 agreement was
reached on thirteen projects for economic and technical cooperation
(eleven to be started by mid-1964) and twelve for technical assistance
under the loan. A good deal of the work is to be undertaken near the
Chinese border and the Chinese Government must now have many
detailed surveys of both military and economic value.

Indonesia, whose relations with China in recent years have blown
hot and cold, has benefited from a moratorium on its trade debts, a
$11 million, 2.5 per cent, credit repayable over ten years to buy
rice and cotton piecegoods and, more recently, a $30 million loan,
again carrying 2.5 per cent interest a year, and repayable over
fifteen years,to buy textile machinery. Indonesia, like Ceylon, is
slow to put plans into practice and Chinese aid has not yet had much
influence on the level of output. There are reports that China has
offered substantial help in the development of the Indonesian petroleum industry; these are plausible but for the present China seems
to be more actively interested in the opportunities for taking part
in the development of Saharan oil.

A Bridgehead in Africa

With the exception of Egypt, which received Swiss francs 20
million ($4.7 million) as a gift to help it over the Suez crisis,
economic aid to Africa did not get under way until 1960. Not unexpectedly Ghana, Guinea and Mali were the first countries south of the
Sahara to be favoured; all were given long-term, interest-free,
loans to finance development projects and technical assistance,

repayment to be in local currency or another currency acceptable to
China or, in the case of Ghana,in kind. The agreement with Guinea
provided for the visits of so many Chinese experts that President
Nasser is said to have warned M. Sekou Toure of the inconveniences
of playing host to large numbers of Communist experts. According
to the Chinese news agency the first factories - to make matches
and cigarettes - built with Chinese help were "emerging from the
swamps of the Guinea coast" towards the end of 1963 and were
expected to go into production during 1964; when in full operation
they are designed to meet all domestic demand and provide a surplus
for export. The Ghanaian Government was promised a cotton spinnery
and weavery and technical help with developing rice cultivation,
fisheries and craft industries. Mali, too, has received technical
assistance on agricultural problems and is to get plant and equipment.

The most recent aid to be given - to Syria, Algeria, Somalia
and Zanzibar - is patently political in intention. In Somalia
the Chinese are bidding against both the Russians and the West; they
have given a grant of £1 million ($2.8 million) to replace the British
subsidy to the Somali budget and an interest-free loan equal to $20
million to finance development. Chinese technical experts are
reported to be scouring the country for suitable projects on which
to spend the money in the hopes of showing themselves more efficient
than the Soviets, who have already been in the field for two years
with little to show for their pains. This unusual activity is said to
have stimulated the U.S. to seek more effective means of expending
its $6 million aid to Somalia.

Aid to Syria and Algeria is almost certainly prompted by a wish
to contain Soviet influence, though in Algeria as in Cuba the Chinese
have been unable to match Russian generosity dollar for dollar. The
$50 million Chinese loan to Algeria in October 1963 came just a
month after the Russians had given double that sum. In helping
Syria the Chinese purpose is presumably to counter growing Soviet
influence in Iraq and Egypt and to prevent the formation of a Middle
Eastern bloc under Russian tutelage. The $500,000 so far promised
to Zanzibar is said to be the forerunner of a proper agreement
covering aid and technical assistance, which will no doubt more than
pay for itself in political nuisance value since the island is a far
better base for operations in eastern and south-eastern Africa than
is Somalia.

IS IT WORTH IT?

The Chinese often make play out of the fact that their aid has no

strings attached; but in the accepted meaning of the term it is rarely
untied. With few exceptions, Chinese loans are to be used to buy
Chinese goods and services, though there may have been instances
where East European machinery formed part of Chinese deliveries –
it is said that one reason why projects in Nepal were hanging fire
was that China was no longer able to obtain the necessary equipment
from East Europe. However, in general recipients of aid are restricted to equipment that the Chinese themselves can make in excess of
their own requirements, which means largely that for the textile and
light industries. While the establishment of such industries may
permit considerable import saving by the receiving country, this
must often be at the expense of China itself – a factor which no
doubt causes considerable annoyance in Peking.

The terms on which aid is given, in so far as they are known,
are not onerous. The time allowed for repayment is normally
generous and the method of repaying not necessarily burdensome,
though in some recent African agreements China left itself the
opportunity to require settlement in a third currency. The policy
in respect of interest charges is somewhat puzzling; it would seem
that since 1960 no interest-bearing loans have been made – Burma
for example got its big 1961 loan free of interest but had to pay 2.5
per cent on an earlier one. Because of this timing, the payment of
interest is confined to Asian countries (and to Hungary) while the
Africans have got off scot-free. The Asian Communists are not
absolved from interest payment on all the money they are lent though
in general they pay 1 per cent, Mongolia alone being charged 2.5
per cent. While interest payments may have been waived recently,
it is noticeable that few outright grants have been made since the
early days of aid-giving.

The benefits that accrue to the recipients of Chinese aid are hard
to assess as yet; as we have seen some of the factories that have
been established have not so far proved economic while others seem
to be working satisfactorily. In general the Chinese seem alive to
the need to make the most of their small resources by avoiding
prestige spending and concentrating on projects that will be, or could
be, of genuine value to the recipient: any road in Yemen is after all
better than none and textile factories are an early requirement of any
developing country. Only in the case of near neighbours does aid
seem sometimes to be designed to help China rather than the recipient.
By and large, however, all aid to development is welcome and the
Chinese by sharpening competition among donors may enable recipients to get more and on better terms.

Time has yet to show whether Chinese technical assistance,
particularly in agriculture, repays the cost of entertaining large
numbers of Chinese experts over a long period. Agreements covering

this subject are signed with all major aid projects and exchanges of
personnel between China and the other signatory are often extensive.
Apart from agriculture, advice is offered on forestry, fisheries,
geology, transport and a host of industries. Such agreements are
not confined to aid recipients but are made with all the Communist
countries and, despite growing coolness, protocols on the exchange
of scientific and technical information during 1963 were signed with
the U.S.S.R. and all the East Europeans,and exchanges of experts,
it would seem, continue unabated.

Once in the aid race China will certainly stay there and undoubtedly step up its contribution to the maximum of its ability. Offers
of substantial aid to a number of other countries are outstanding -
Iraq, Pakistan, Nigeria - and it seems unlikely that Premier
Chou will have undertaken his African and Asian tours empty-
handed except for the token sum given to Zanzibar; but for the
foreseeable future China will have to dispense largesse thriftily.
As the range of plant that China can make broadens so will the
range of its aid widen, but in many branches of industry its own
needs will absorb all available resources for some years to come.
It may be hazarded that the aid effort will be stepped up in Africa
and perhaps extended to the mainland of Latin America. Unless
Indonesian oil claims Chinese interest there seems little reason to
expect that the pot will be kept more than simmering in Asia;
Burma, Ceylon and Nepal have yet to absorb existing allocations;
India is not a potential recipient and Pakistan may be chary of
accepting more than limited help with small industries, for fear of
offending its larger benefactors. Any opportunities to help Eastern
Europe would no doubt be eagerly seized upon to spite the U.S.S.R.,
while the Asian Communists must be kept in the Chinese camp and
prevented from sinking into the quagmire of their own inefficiency.

CHAPTER NEW
DIRECTIONS

We now come to the problem of summing up and expressing an
opinion, for it can be no more than that, on the likely course of
China's foreign trade over the remainder of the present decade. To
look further in any but the broadest terms seems otiose when a
single political decision could change the whole framework within
which the trade is conducted. For in the last resort the foreign
trade of any Communist country is governed by political and not
commercial principles. This does not imply that political considerations alone determine China's foreign trade any more than it
implies that politics play no part in Western trade; nor is it
suggested that political decisions can alter China's basic resources.
But a Chinese Government could, for example, if it so wished
impose a policy of autarky in a manner and at a speed beyond the
powers of a democratic administration. That it would do so before
the end of the 'sixties is unlikely; but autarky is one of a number
of long-term possibilities that China's planners may consider when
formulating policy to take account of the changing structure of the
economy as industrialization progresses.

At present rumour and speculation thrive on the absence of
factual data about China's economy and external trade. Such facts
or near facts as emerge from the mainland are too often interpreted
in the light of personal prejudice rather than in any wider context;
motives are attributed to the policy-makers on the slenderest
evidence and China becomes, à choix, a gentle giant or menacing
monster. In an attempt to avoid over-hasty judgments based on the
latest handout from Peking or rumour from Hong Kong, we try in
the following paragraphs to see China's foreign trade as one aspect
of the continuing process of developing the country's economy.

PRIORITIES AND PROBLEMS

To forecast the course of China's economy while the Peking
Government maintains silence about its long-term plans is not easy.
The reassessment of priorities that followed the agricultural disasters was clearly a majority and not a unanimous decision of the
powers that be; the continued secrecy of the National People's

Congress meetings and the fact that planning remains on an annual basis suggest that it has so far been impossible to reach general agreement on economic policy. For the present, the pragmatists have the upper hand, but the theoreticians are not beaten. In the short term, the choice was between devoting resources to improving the food situation or accepting the Malthusian solution to a population multiplying faster than the means of subsistence.

To continue to emphasize agriculture at the expense of industry inevitably implies acceptance of a much slower rate of progress than that achieved during the First Five-Year Plan and it is ideologically unorthodox. There are, however, some indications that present priorities, originally established in response to a critical situation, will out-last that situation and remain in force until at least the later years of the current decade. The nature of the industrial plant recently ordered in Western Europe and Japan supports this view. With the exception of the L/D smelter that may be acquired from Austria, all the plants are designed to raise the output of agriculture or of light industries serving the consumer market; if, as is rumoured, a petrochemical complex is set up with foreign help, its primary task will be to supply raw materials to the plastics industry. Delivery of the plant already ordered will take place over the coming two and a half to three years so that full output will not be achieved until 1968 at the earliest, and the full yield of the investment in fertilizer capacity will not be realized until still later.

In the longer term, however, - that is, beyond the next five years - it would be surprising indeed (in the absence of a change in regime) if industry, and in particular heavy industry, did not come into its own again and resume its place as priority number one. A switch could, of course, be induced earlier either by a change in the faction in power, or by a series of favourable harvests - though after their recent experiences the present leaders would be chary of another forward stride that might result in two steps back.

The structural problems that the policy-makers have to solve fall into three, interrelated, groups: population (and labour), agriculture, investment. First and foremost they must make an asset and not a liability of the one factor of production that China has in abundance, labour. It is as yet unproven whether the country's immense reservoir of human power will turn out to be a source of strength or merely a continued drag on progress; even its precise size remains unknown. The initial results of the 1953 census showed a population on the mainland of China of 583 million, but the total was later revised to 595.6 million. Ten Great Years gives a 1957 population of 656.6 million at the year's end, implying a natural increase of something slightly over 2 per cent a year. A figure of "about 2 per cent" was mentioned late in 1963 by Chou En-lai as the average annual natural increase for the country as a whole; on this basis, and accepting the revised total for 1953, China's population would be 740 million in 1964 and over 830 million in 1970. It is, however, possible that the 2 per cent rate has not been maintained consistently over the last few years (during the food crisis fertility may have been reduced and the death rate will surely have risen); Chinese leaders even now continue to speak of a population of 650-odd million and on no occasion has a figure above 700 million yet been mentioned. The lowest natural increase regarded as likely by Western demographers is 1.6 per cent a year and this would give total of 710 million in 1964 and 780 million in 1970. As a working hypothesis, then, it may be assumed that the present population is about 720 million and that by 1970 it will have reached some 800 million.

To feed and clothe and provide work for such numbers is no mean task, even if no attempt is made to raise the standard of living, and there is evidence that the authorities are once again exercised about the problem of population control. The birth control campaign initiated in the early days of the First Plan reached its peak in 1957 only to be dropped like a hot potato under the influence of the Great Leap illusion that Mao had set the country firmly on the path of fast, self-sustained growth. It is unlikely that the brash, frontal attack on the problem met with anything but strong resistance and incomprehension from the peasant population, though some town-dwellers may have been induced to restrict their families. The present campaign is more limited and devious; though the use of contraceptives is again being urged, more stress is put on encouraging later marriages and on sterilization, and economic inducements and disincentives are used to establish an   optimum family size of two or three children. It would seem that, as in other matters, the authorities have abandoned hope of swift and spectacular results.

Can this enormous, growing and young population be so employed as to produce surplus to its own requirements and thus provide the wherewithal to finance the greater investment that will raise living standards, or must its ability to consume always tend to outstrip its ability to produce? Is the solution usually favoured in an under-developed country - the absorption of surplus labour by industry - applicable in China? The Chinese Government's first experiment in large-scale organization of agriculture in order to release man-power for labour-intensive investment in industry was not a success, and demonstrated very clearly how small a proportion of the labour force industry could absorb effectively, at least in the short run. One of the first post-Leap crisis measures was to send back to the countryside as many as possible of the 16 million alleged to have

flocked to the towns in 1958, for whom by 1960 there was no work and
no food unless they produced it themselves.[1.] But can agriculture
simultaneously take the strain of providing work for the growing labour
force, food for the additional population, and the savings needed to
finance both investment in industry to the point where industry can
finance its own growth and investment in the land - inevitably slow-
yielding? If it is organized in large-scale units employing a great
deal of labour, it may fail to produce much over and above its own
needs unless the incentives are more attractive than they have been
up to the present. If individual enterprise is permitted, even on a
limited scale, production is likely to rise but savings will be difficult to tap and to direct. If farming is based on large-scale mech-
anized units, production will almost certainly rise and with it
surpluses that can easily be employed in such a way as to further
state investment plans; but this will leave the problem of employment
unresolved.

Outside intervention could be of help in one respect: foreign aid
could supplement domestic savings in financing investment. That it
will do so to any appreciable extent seems, however, most improbable - not only because no international lender, private or official,
has anything to gain from helping China (which cannot of course call
on any of the international agencies such as the World Bank) but
because the Peking Government believes in the virtues of self-
reliance. In the past the Communist regime has had minimal aid
from its allies; in the future the best that it can look forward to are
ordinary trade credits and the medium-term loans normally accorded
in international trade on the sale of plant. These may slightly defer
the impact of the cost of a large investment, but not necessarily to
the point at which the investment is itself productive.

Even an all-powerful Communist Government has no quick answer
to structural problems of this magnitude and must learn to live with
them. China's policy-makers are evidently not prepared to adopt
Stalin's cold-blooded method of industrializing at the cost of millions
of peasant lives; nor will they accept, let alone ask for, outside
help on a scale commensurate with their needs. Each of the major
problems is being attacked with determination and method, but for

---

1. It is interesting to note that Ten Great Years claims only a 45
per cent increase in the number of industrial workers between 1953
and 1957, to a total of 9 million in the latter year. Annual increases
are given as follows: 1952-53: 1.2 million; 1953-54, 220,000; 1954-
55, 69,000; 1955-56, 2.1 million; 1956-57, 382,000. The increase
claimed for 1958 is the ridiculous figure of 16.6 million, to a total
of 25.6 million.

the time being the struggle is being waged on a nineteenth century not
a twentieth century time-scale; birth control, labour training schemes,
greater irrigation and land reclamation, rationalization of existing
industrial investment and concentration of resources will yield no
quick results. Because it is a law unto itself, it may be easier for
China than for other developing countries to get away with a low growth
rate, but Chinese leaders must continue to search for ways of achieving and maintaining a rate of increase in physical output that is well
above the natural population increase.

LITTLE TO SPARE

If in the short run the Peking Government must favour agriculture
over industry, consumption at the expense of investment, in order to
establish a sound foundation for massive investment in industry in the
longer term, what effect will this have on the size and composition of
China's foreign trade? In the absence of foreign aid the size of the
import market will be determined very largely by the country's ability
to export goods; gold and silver may be used from time to time in
settlement of debts but are unlikely to be exported regularly in significant quantities; and remittances of Overseas Chinese will continue
to provide a useful invisible income. None of these items, however,
provides a rapidly expanding source of foreign exchange so that
resources available to pay for imports are not likely to be substantially
greater in the middle and late 'sixties than they were in the good years
in the 'fifties. In each of the three years 1958, 1959 and 1960 exports
yielded roughly $2 billion, according to U.N. calculations; by 1962
the figure may have fallen rather short of $1.5 billion, recovering to
perhaps $1.6 billion in 1963. Since the 1963 harvest was not parti-
cularly good, 1964 exports are unlikely to exceed $1.75 billion, and
may well not reach this figure; and, barring exceptional harvests, it
will probably not be until the end of the 'sixties, when the newly
imported plants will be in full operation, that exports will again
exceed $2 billion.

A sizable part of these export proceeds is, moreover, already
committed; there are the down payments to be made on the $60-odd
million worth of plant ordered from Japan and Western Europe, and
as soon as debts to Russia have been settled in 1965, repayment will
start of Western and Japanese credits, which will presumably continue until about 1970. In addition, commitments already entered into
with regard to grain purchases could extend until end-1967 unless
credits are repaid ahead of schedule.

With forward commitments already fairly heavy, it seems unlikely that China will continue to place orders abroad for plant on the same scale that it has done in recent months. Some of the deals at present rumoured may be concluded, but it would not be surprising if the authorities then concentrated on obtaining as much technical assistance and know-how as possible without committing themselves to further large expenditure until perhaps 1967 or 1968. This spasmodic ordering of equipment is quite consistent with forward planning of the internal economy and seems to have been employed earlier in dealings with the U.S.S.R. The orders placed in the later 'sixties should be a guide to the trend of economic policy in the 'seventies, if by then the Chinese are indeed thinking once again in terms of concentrating resources on the capital goods sector.

For the present, basic materials for industry and agriculture will continue to have a high priority on the import list. Among the goods that will have to be bought, perhaps in increasing quantities, is rubber both to meet growing domestic needs and to provide tyres, rubber footwear and other products for export. Purchases of cotton and wool, too, seem likely to rise at least during the next three or four years. Thereafter, the outlook is less clear; efforts to raise local cotton production may prove successful and when the newly-bought synthetic fibre plants come into operation, the textile industry will probably be encouraged to make the greatest possible use of man-made fibres at the expense of the natural products. Special steels and some non-ferrous metals will certainly continue to figure quite prominently among imports for some years to come; so too will petroleum products. It would be reasonable to suppose that domestic production of fertilizers, believed to be about 2.7 million tons in 1963, will be supplemented by fairly big imports at least until the new plants come into operation and perhaps longer. Even when all four plants now on order are in full production, domestic capacity will fall far short of estimated requirements of 24 million tons a year (a level of consumption that could naturally only be reached after years of carefully planned build-up). Other essentials for agriculture, insecticides, high-quality seed and breeding stock, are comparatively cheap in relation to the returns that they yield and will no doubt be purchased as need arises.

Grain imports are clearly not to cease before 1967 and may continue longer, though how much is bought over and above existing commitments is partly a matter of the size of future harvests. Until domestic agricultural production has reached much larger proportions and is capable of ensuring an adequate diet year in year out for the rising population, it is probably more advantageous for China to remain in the world market continuously and to build up contacts and reputation rather than to fall back on it in times of need only. (The massive incursion of the U.S.S.R. into both wheat and sugar markets

in recent months may give the Peking authorities cause for some
anxiety; had this preceded China's own crises, the terms for obtaining Western food might have been very much harsher). In normal
years the balance sheet of China's trade in foodstuffs is not at all
unfavourable: cheap foodgrains are imported, expensive rice is
exported; low–cost coarse grains feed a profitable trade in meat
and meat products. Two other foodstuffs which might come to
feature prominently in the import bill, for political if no better
reasons, are coffee and cocoa; they could be the price of getting
Chinese men and materials accepted in West Africa and Latin
America.

Imports of machinery, as distinct from complete plant, are
likely to rise to the maximum extent allowed by the foreign exchange
position after other priorities have been met - but the sum involved
will hardly be large. Buying will be at the same time extremely
selective and very wide-ranging; key equipment will be bought for
anything from the mining industry to the lightest of consumer goods
industries if it is regarded as essential to the fulfilment of plans.
Agricultural machinery may also be imported, but probably to provide prototypes for Chinese factories to copy rather than in quantity.
A market for other types of finished goods does not exist and will
not be permitted to develop unless political expediency demands it:
it might, for example, bolster Albania's amour propre to sell textiles to China; it may be marginally more advantageous to accept
Indonesian knick-knacks rather than to accord yet another moratorium on trade debts. But no Western industrialist need hope to
purvey consumer goods to the Chinese market.

The composition of China's exports cannot undergo any quick
change however economic policy may veer: the trend towards
processed goods and away from raw materials will continue but
is unlikely to gather momentum before the 'seventies; diversification
will be a slow and arduous process. But the diversion of trade from
the U.S.S.R. and East Europe may make it appear to the non-
Communist world that Chinese exports have suddenly grown in volume
and variety. As heretofore the "purpose of exporting is importing",
and this will be achieved as it has been in the past partly by compen-
satory deliveries against imports, partly by building up surpluses in
one area to cover deficits in another. The primary determinant of
the volume of exports in any one year will continue to be the previous
year's harvest. Not only does agriculture directly provide a large
volume of exports, but it also supplies many of the raw materials
needed for processing by the various branches of the textile and
light industries. One the other hand, as industrial output expands
more minerals will be diverted from the export to the home market.

NO MORE LEANING TO ONE SIDE

The changes in the composition of imports implied by the new economic policy are nothing compared with the revolution that is taking place in the sources of supply as a result of the Sino-Soviet conflict. China's leaders appear to have been cured once and for all of their early belief that the U.S.S.R. and its satellites could provide most of what was required from abroad on the most advantageous terms obtainable, and to have accepted the fact that foreign trade is best conducted on a world-wide scale, with due weight accorded to commercial considerations. This does not mean that China's trade with the Communist Bloc will shrivel away to nothing or that politics will no longer play any part in foreign trade; but for the time being China's leaders are concerned to organise the country's international trade in such a way that it will make the maximum contribution to internal growth, even if this means jettisoning some cherished ideological theories.

It seems probable that trade with the Soviet Union itself will settle at a very low level. Total turnover dropped from $2 billion in 1959 to $750 million in 1962, when Soviet imports from China were more than double its exports there. This Chinese surplus (in repayment of debts, it will be recalled) was probably smaller in 1963 and 1964 and will disappear after next year. In the second half of the decade Sino-Soviet exchanges are thus likely to be in balance at perhaps no more than $200 million to $225 million each way. Neither side will be prepared to put itself out for the other: the U.S.S.R. will not accord even short-term credit; China will be unwilling to sell worthwhile goods to Russia that could be disposed of elsewhere. The already small natural base for trade will be further limited by man-made obstructions. This will not, however, necessarily be true of trade with all the East Europeans; those still tied to Russia's apron strings may eschew dealings with China but the freer spirits will not. Sino-Rumanian trade, for example, should certainly increase for Rumania has petroleum, and oil-drilling and refining equipment and know-how that China wants and would be willing to pay for in acceptable goods. The same may happen with Hungary or Poland, but trade with the area as a whole (though perhaps not with each individual country) will be kept in balance.

Western Europe and Japan have already benefited from the diversion of trade from the U.S.S.R.: Britain, France, Italy, the Netherlands and Japan have all received orders for at least one major plant and are being visited by a number of Chinese technical missions gaining information and possibly framing recommendations

for further purchases. These countries will also remain a source of
supply of basic materials such as steel and fertilizers, and may grow
in importance in this sphere too. They should in addition share with
the East Europeans still trading actively with China the bulk of
machinery purchases that will be made in the next few years.
Canada and Australia could have participated in this trade were not
China already so heavily in debt to them on account of food purchases.

There will be less change in other sources of supply: South East
Asia will continue to provide rubber; the Middle East and North
Africa will be the principal sources of cotton; petroleum supplies,
once a near monopoly of the U.S.S.R., may, however, be sought
in the Sahara or perhaps Indonesia rather than the Middle East as
hitherto. Food will come mainly as now from Canada and Australia
but in coming years Latin America seems likely to replace South
Africa and Rhodesia as a maize supplier, and Western Europe may
drop out altogether as a food supplier because there are other more
important purchases to be made there. In all, by the end of the
decade the non-Communist world should again be providing well over
half of all China's imports.

The diversion of exports will have to be as great as that of imports,
for there will be no point in accumulating surpluses within the Soviet
orbit once debts are paid off. This will be a considerable problem.
As far as possible, imports from Western Europe and Japan will be
offset by exports of Chinese goods required in those countries; but
the demand for traditional exports is limited in range and inelastic,
and any attempts to diversify into sales of manufactured goods would
immediately run up against physical controls on imports - even
before difficulties were encountered on account of poor quality and
design. The focal points of the export drive that China must mount
in the next few years will be, as ever, Hong Kong and Macao, Asian
members of the Sterling Area with whom it is possible to earn a
surplus and African members of the Sterling Area and Franc Zone
who can be milked to pay for imports from Europe.

How uncomfortable Chinese competition will be for established
traders is hard to predict. As far as concerns basic materials
temporarily surplus to China's own needs, such as steel and
cement, it could be devastating in a single market, if short-lived,
since China would have no hesitation in under-cutting the lowest
bidder if it seemed advantageous to do so. But this piratical behaviour may be less rewarding in the case of more diverse products and ones in which it is intended to build up a long-term
market, such as machinery or consumer goods. Chinese corporations scored some successes with textiles in West Africa and South
East Asia in 1958, but these were shortlived since the economic
crisis of the early 'sixties cut into supplies. China has yet to

establish a reputation for its products that will stand the test with goods from the industrialized countries; if it could make simple and sturdy agricultural implements and machinery at low cost these could find ready markets, but even in the underdeveloped world cheap and shoddy is soon recognized and rejected.

In general China gives the impression of being very well informed on world raw material and commodity markets both as buyer and seller, but it has much to learn about international trade in manufactures after its years of isolation within the Soviet orbit. Its enlarged quota for sensitive goods in the Canadian market will no doubt provide some salutary lessons about the standards expected by sophisticated consumers and teach the sharpness of Japanese and Hong Kong competition. Indeed, it is hard to envisage how in present circumstances China could compete effectively in many light industrial products with its Far Eastern neighbours, who are alert to every change in taste in their overseas markets and one of whom has in addition a discriminating home market. The fact that the Chinese market has had to make do with many sub-standard manufactures in recent years will do the country's export trade no good; and though domestic consumers are now being asked for their views on the products available in the shops it will take some time before factories put into practice suggestions for improvements. Nevertheless, by hook or by crook, China must export and it must learn to meet the requirements of customers in South East Asia and Africa.

As China is drawn further into the non-Communist trading world, there seems a good chance that its leaders will be less inclined than they were in the 'fifties to use foreign trade as a weapon to gain political ends - particularly among the industrialized nations. (The extent to which the ideological battle within the Communist orbit may be waged with economic weapons need not concern us here). For some years to come, China's position will be too vulnerable to permit behaviour likely to rebound in sanctions; the industrialized nations could more easily dispense with the Chinese market than China with supplies of Western plant and equipment. No doubt pressure groups for trade with China, such as the 'friendly' firms in Japan and the 48 Group in Britain, will continue to receive encouragement, and industrialists will be reminded constantly of the potential of the Chinese market. They may be pushed into making representations to their governments about the revision of the embargo list; but a direct attempt to influence the course of elections, similar to that in Japan in 1958, seems improbable.

How far the Peking Government will attempt to play off one country against another by its distribution of orders between Japan and Western Europe and within Western Europe is an interesting question. The recent orders for plant were not preceded by any calls for the

submission of competitive tenders; the Chinese authorities apparently
decided what plant they wanted from each country and then approached
the manufacturers with the offer of a contract, over the details of
which they negotiated with extreme toughness and pertinacity but without apparently the threat of withdrawal and placement elsewhere.
With more direct knowledge of conditions in each country, they may
well in future abandon this rather secretive approach in favour of a
more normal method of using competition to secure the most
advantageous terms. An intriguing omission from the list of
countries with which orders for plant have been placed is Western
Germany; this may be fortuitous, it might on the other hand be part
of a softening up process.

In the underdeveloped world the temptation to use trade and aid as
political weapons is greater. Chinese purchasing policy will be
dictated first and foremost by the needs of its own economy; but if
political capital can be made by relieving a country of a surplus at
comparatively little cost, this will no doubt be done. Grand gestures
with regard to either trade or aid are for the present out of the
question, but there is little reason to suppose that China's aid effort
will in the future be any less effective in relation to its size than it
has been in the past; it will be used to the maximum discomfiture
of the Soviet Union and the West alike and to the benefit of China in
the political, economic or strategic sphere as the case may be.

For how long the Chinese giant will continue to play a dwarf's
part in international trade is a question that is at present unanswer-
able. In time it may come to dominate certain sectors of trade,
certain countries or commodities, and to impose upon them its own
trading ethics and practices, which may be very different from those
currently accepted; it may on the other hand retreat into near self-
sufficiency. For the next five to ten years, however, it may well
fit into the existing framework of international trade and,viewed
objectively, be a less hazardous and more credit-worthy trading
partner than many an underdeveloped member of the non-Communist
world that is less thrifty of its assets. There is nothing in China's
known resources, human or material, to suggest that the country
can in the next decade achieve and sustain a rate of economic growth
so rapid as to require a level of foreign trade that would alter more
than marginally existing trends in the development of the volume and
composition of world trade as a whole.

STATISTICAL
APPENDIX

APPENDIX I: COMPOSITION AND DIRECTION OF CHINA'S TRADE: 1931, 1936, 1946, 1948

Percentages	1931		1936		1946		1948	
	Exports	Imports	Exports	Imports	Exports	Imports	Exports	Imports
A. Composition								
Food & drink	15.7	22.6	24.7	11.0	14.6	18.0[a]	18.0	13.4[a]
Raw materials	37.7	21.7	35.8	13.4	41.9	24.7[a]	19.4	27.8[a]
Semi-manufactures	32.5	19.7	23.2	22.3	23.6	14.3[a]	25.9[b]	16.4[a]
Manufactures	13.6	34.4	16.3	44.2	19.9	43.0[a]	36.7	42.4[a]
Miscellaneous	0.5	1.6	–	9.1	–	–	–	–
Total	100.0	100.0	100.0	100.0	100.0	100.0[a]	100.0	100.0[a]
B. Direction								
Japan	27.4	20.0	14.5	16.3	3.1	0.4[c]	5.5	0.9[c]
U.S.A.	13.2	22.2	26.4	19.6	38.7	57.2[c]	20.1	48.4[c]
Hong Kong	16.3	15.3	15.1	1.9	28.2	4.5[c]	15.0	1.5[c]
U.K.	7.1	8.3	9.2	11.7	4.4	4.6[c]	3.9[d]	8.1[c]
Others	36.0	34.2	34.6	50.5	25.6	33.3[c]	55.5	41.1[c]
Total	100.0	100.0	100.0	100.0	100.0	100.0[c]	100.0	100.0[c]

a. Total imports, including U.N.R.R.A. supplies etc.   b. Result of export drive following huge aid imports of raw cotton.   c. Commercial imports.   d. Of which S.E. Asia 20.2.

Source Yu-Kwei Cheng, Foreign Trade and Industrial Development of China, adapted from tables on pp 48–49, 177–8.

APPENDIX II: VOLUME OF OUTPUT OF
SELECTED PRODUCTS UP TO 1957

Products	Unit	Pre-1949 peak	1949	1952	1953	1957
Agricultural						
Grain	mn tons	138.7	108.1	154.4	156.9	185.0
a. Rice (paddy)	" "	57.4	48.7	68.5	71.3	86.8
b. Wheat	" "	23.3	13.8	18.1	18.3	23.6
c. Coarse grains	" "	51.7	25.8	51.8	50.7	52.7
d. Potatoes[a]	" "	6.4	9.9	16.4	16.7	21.9
Cotton	'000 tons	849	445	1,304	1,175	1,640
Soya beans	mn tons	11.3	5.1	9.5	9.9	10.1
Groundnuts	'000 tons	...	1,268	2,316	2,127	2,571
Rapeseed	" "	...	734	932	879	888
Sugar beet	" "	...	195	479	505	1,501
Sugar cane	" "	...	2,642	7,116	7,209	10,392
Cured tobacco	" "	...	43	222	213	256
Tea	" "	...	41	83	85	112
Mineral						
Copper[b]	'000 tons	...	4	8	11	20
Antimony[b]	" "	...	4	8	10	14
Tin concentrates	" "	...	5	6	6	16
Lead[b]	" "	...	4	6	10	20
Zinc[b]	" "	...	...	...	...	15
Tungsten[b]	" "	...	6	10	12	9
Coal	mn tons	62	32	66	70	130
Crude petroleum	'000 tons	321	121	436	622	1,458
Industrial						
Steel	'000 tons	923	158	1,349	1,774	5,350
Pig iron	" "	1,801	252	1,929	2,234	5,936
Electric power	bn kwh	7	4	7	9	19
Cement	'000 tons	2,290	660	2,860	3,880	6,860
Sulphuric acid	" "	180	40	190	260	632
Chemical fertilizer	" "	227	27	181	226	631
Power machinery	'000 h.p.	...	10	35	144	690
Electric motors	'000 kw	...	61	639	918	1,455
Locomotives	units	-	-	20	10	167

APPENDIX II: (Continued)

Products	Unit	Pre-1949 peak	1949	1952	1953	1957
Industrial (continued)						
Motor vehicles	units	–	–	–	–	7,500
Bicycles	'000 units	...	14	80	165	806
Cotton cloth	mn metres	2,790	1,890	3,830	4,690	5,050
Paper	'000 tons	120	228	539	667	998
Sugar	" "	414	199	451	638	864

... Not available. – Nil.

a. In terms of grain equivalent. b. Metal content.

Sources: SSB, Ten Great Years; U. N. Statistical Yearbook.

APPENDIX III: TRADE OF SELECTED
A. EXPORTS

$ million	1953	1954	1955	1956	1957	
Western Europe						
Austria	–	1.3	1.8	7.4	7.8	1
Belgium/ Luxemburg	1.4	0.5	7.0	21.4	22.2	2
Denmark	0.3	0.3	0.1	3.1	0.7	3
Finland	5.4	6.6	12.5	7.5	4.7	4
France	12.3^a	8.7^a	7.1^a	22.8^a	21.8^a	5
Italy	2.7^a	6.2^a	5.7^a	10.4^a	14.7	6
Netherlands	3.9	1.0	2.9	6.0	5.5	7
Norway	0.9	–	–	2.3	1.8	8
Sweden	2.7	0.7	1.8	6.1	27.0	9
Switzerland	26.4^b	23.2^b	23.8^b	35.4^b	43.4^b	10
U.K.	28.6	19.4	22.3	30.2	34.1	11
W. Germany	25.0	21.5	26.2	37.1	47.6	12
Eastern Europe						
Albania	...	...	–	0.8	0.1	13
Bulgaria	5.3	...	4.6	5.1	4.0	14
Czecho- slovakia	...	...	57.7	64.7	81.3	15
E. Germany	60.3	99.5	97.5	94.9	105.8	16
Hungary	29.6	...	36.5	31.1	29.4	17
Poland	31.0	37.0	34.8	50.3	44.9	18
Rumania	...	...	...	...	...	19
U.S.S.R.	697.0	826.0	748.4	733.1	544.1	20
Yugoslavia	–	–	–	4.4	4.0	21
Asia						
Iraq	–	–	0.2	–	–	22
Syria	...	0.6	0.2	1.6	10.5	23
Burma	1.3	0.1	17.5	15.1	9.1	24
Ceylon	50.8	46.5	25.5	38.3	35.2	25
Hong Kong	94.5	68.4	31.8	23.8	21.6	26
India	2.5	3.7	14.3	8.0	7.7	27
Pakistan	7.2^a	26.1^a	31.7^a	15.9^a	9.5	28
Cambodia	–	–	–	–	–	29

COUNTRIES WITH CHINA 1953-1963
TO CHINA

	1958	1959	1960	1961	1962	1962	1963	Jan.
								to:
1	14.3	14.4	12.9	2.1	1.1	1.1	1.1	Dec.
2	41.5	33.5	44.8	10.3	8.0	8.0	9.5	"
3	4.3	3.5	2.1	3.8	3.6	3.6	0.6	"
4	8.4	16.5	6.5	6.0	5.1	5.1	5.7	"
5	38.1	39.8	53.3	36.4	43.3	43.3	58.4	"
6	32.7	36.4	40.0	29.9	19.0	19.0	19.4	"
7	11.9	11.2	6.9	4.1	3.6	3.6	12.8	"
8	4.8	7.6	4.1	5.0	0.9	0.9	3.4	"
9	17.6[b]	14.4[b]	13.2	7.5	4.8	4.1	3.6	Nov.
10	31.4[b]	34.9[b]	8.1	5.3	3.6	3.6	4.0	Dec.
11	76.3	69.4	87.6	36.5	24.1	24.1	37.4	"
12	162.4	128.7	95.4	30.5	31.1	31.1	15.4	"
13	0.8	0.8	...	...	...	...	...	
14	11.0	6.3	7.5	...	...	...	...	
15	109.2	99.6	109.3	34.0	11.9	...	...	
16	133.3	106.4	97.1	55.1	...	...	...	
17	57.4	39.9	39.1	28.0	...	...	...	
18	72.2	42.9	50.0	26.7	15.1	13.0	7.7	Sept.
19	25.9	29.4	33.3	9.0	...	...	...	
20	634.9	954.0	817.1	367.3	233.5	...	...	
21	4.5	1.4	1.1	-	-	-	-	Nov.
22	-	2.2	1.5	1.5	4.0	...	...	
23	6.7	0.1	...	12.1	7.2	3.6	16.0	Sept.
24	3.0	0.4	7.8	37.4	1.2	...	...	
25	16.3	16.3	25.4	17.4	28.0	21.9[c]	24.9[c]	Oct.
26	27.3	20.0	21.1	17.3	14.9	14.9	12.3	Dec.
27	7.2	16.4	11.8	0.4	0.4	0.4	-	Oct.
28	7.6	0.7	14.7	10.0	1.6	1.6	9.0	Aug.
29	-	1.5	1.3	0.7	...	...	...	

APPENDIX III: (Continued)

A. EXPORTS

$ million	1953	1954	1955	1956	1957	
<u>Asia</u> (continued)						
Indonesia	–	2.8	6.5	11.7	26.3	1
Japan	4.5	19.1	28.6	67.3	60.5	2
Malaya/ Singapore	1.8	6.4	4.2	7.8	24.2	3
Sarawak	–	–	–	–	–	4
Sabah	...	...	...	–	1.8	5
<u>America</u>						
Canada	–	0.1	1.0	2.5	1.4	6
Argentina	–	4.5	0.7	0.8	0.7	7
Brazil	1.0	2.6	4.6	–	–	8
Cuba	–	1.2	0.4	–	–	9
Uruguay	...	–	–	–	2.6	10
<u>Africa</u>						
Egypt	10.4	11.4	24.5	24.2	42.1	11
Sudan	0.1	0.2	0.8	2.5	1.8	12
S. Africa	0.1	0.7	1.2	1.2	2.8	13
Algeria	–	0.7	1.2	–	–	14
Morocco	–	–	–	–	–	15
Tunisia	–	–	–	0.6	–	16
Ghana	–	–	–	–	–	17
Kenya	–	–	0.2	0.2	0.2	18
Uganda	–	–	–	–	2.3	19
Tanganyika	–	–	–	0.3	0.2	20
<u>Australasia</u>						
Australia	4.9	3.2	6.3	10.1	20.5	21
New Zealand	–	–	–	0.4	1.7	22

TO CHINA

	1958	1959	1960	1961	1962	1962	1963	Jan.
								to:
1	43.4	53.1	35.1	36.0	...	...	...	
2	50.6	3.7	2.7	16.7	38.5	38.5	62.4	Dec.
3	38.1	39.8	28.8	4.0	1.2	...	...	
4	0.1	0.1	–	–	–	...	...	
5	0.9	0.4	0.6	0.7	0.5	...	...	
6	8.1	1.8	8.7	122.8	137.0	137.0	96.9	Dec.
7	0.2	0.4	1.6	4.2	...	...	0.6	"
8	7.5	–	0.5	–	–	...	...	
9	–	3.6	0.1	32.1	...	...	...	
10	1.0	2.8	4.3	2.4	0.7	...	...	
11	34.9	33.8	44.5	14.6	19.2	4.4	15.2	Mar.
12	2.1	3.0	9.2	3.9	8.8	1.3	0.2	Apr.
13	7.0	–	9.3	–	5.8	...	...	
14	–	–	...	...	...	...	...	
15	2.6	5.4	6.6	3.7	4.2	...	...	
16	–	0.8	–	0.5	0.2	0.2	–	June
17	–	–	1.4[a]	0.2[a]	1.3[a]	1.2[a]	–	Aug.
18	0.6	0.7	1.0	0.1	0.5	0.5	1.0	Dec.
19	–	–	5.1	9.4	–	–	11.2	"
20	0.7	0.3	0.7	–	–	–	10.4	"
21	27.1	30.1	24.0	160.8	98.6	98.6	209.7	"
22	2.7	7.0	6.5	3.7	3.3	2.2	4.0	Sept.

APPENDIX III: (Continued)

B. IMPORTS

$ million	1953	1954	1955	1956	1957	
Western Europe						
Austria	0.9	0.8	1.2	2.1	2.3	1
Belgium/ Luxemburg	7.2	2.2	1.9	5.0	3.7	2
Denmark	2.0	0.3	0.2	1.4	0.5	3
Finland	1.5	2.8	4.1	2.5	4.8	4
France	11.0[a]	9.4[a]	11.7[a]	14.7[a]	14.6[a]	5
Italy	7.4[a]	2.4[a]	4.1[a]	11.4[a]	6.9	6
Netherlands	15.1	6.2	8.1	11.4	9.8	7
Norway	3.6	2.4	1.9	2.6	1.5	8
Sweden	1.6	1.7	2.3	2.6	3.1	9
Switzerland	16.1[b]	10.9[b]	15.8[b]	19.1[b]	12.5[b]	10
U.K.	17.5	25.1	34.4	35.1	39.8	11
W. Germany	·33.2	36.1	45.9	53.2	41.0	12
Eastern Europe						
Albania	...	...	1.2	4.1	5.9	13
Bulgaria	4.6	...	4.2	5.1	4.6	14
Czecho- slovakia	...	...	60.5	66.4	66.9	15
E. Germany	53.0	67.3	94.1	85.9	88.6	16
Hungary	33.6	...	29.0	28.5	31.3	17
Poland	27.1	29.6	35.2	35.2	37.3	18
Rumania	...	...	...	...	...	19
U.S.S.R.	475.0	545.0	643.5	764.2	738.1	20
Yugoslavia	-	-	-	4.1	7.1	21
Asia						
Iraq	-	-	-	-	-	22
Syria	1.0	0.2	0.2	0.3	0.5	23
Burma ·	1.5	0.5	2.3	22.2	12.5	24
Ceylon	43.9	33.2	16.8	28.1	17.6	25
Hong Kong	150.0	121.1	157.1	181.7	197.9	26
India	1.9[a]	3.2[a]	5.4[a]	17.5[a]	10.2	27
Pakistan	3.3[a]	1.6[a]	0.2[a]	0.5[a]	7.8	28
Cambodia	-	-	-	-	2.3	29

FROM CHINA

	1958	1959	1960	1961	1962	1962	1963	Jan.
								to:
1	2.5	3.2	5.8	3.5	3.6	3.6	3.2	Dec.
2	6.0	8.7	10.0	3.4	4.8	4.8	8.2	"
3	4.0	7.2	10.2	6.6	3.8	3.8	4.2	"
4	3.9	4.7	4.5	2.6	2.1	2.1	3.0	"
5	9.8	16.2	22.9	16.0	16.9	16.9	21.1	"
6	13.7	13.2	24.2	12.3	14.1	14.1	19.2	"
7	17.1	22.1	21.3	15.1	13.9	13.9	15.7	"
8	2.7	2.6	3.1	1.8	1.5	1.5	1.9	"
9	3.8	5.4	5.9	4.3	5.2	4.7	7.2	Nov.
10	11.0[b]	11.6[b]	8.8	9.4	9.9	9.9	10.3	Dec.
11	51.9	55.2	69.6	86.4	64.8	64.8	51.8	"
12	58.5	66.3	69.4	39.7	39.3	39.3	40.8	"
13	1.7	2.4	...	...	...	...	...	
14	7.1	10.6	9.6	...	...	...	...	
15	91.0	95.6	93.3	41.9	25.6	...	...	
16	103.8	112.0	100.0	41.1	...	...	...	
17	33.9	43.8	35.1	17.0	...	...	...	
18	36.3	56.1	46.4	20.7	22.8	15.4	19.8	Sept.
19	16.6	29.9	23.5	19.7	...	...	...	
20	881.3	1,100.3	848.1	551.5	516.3	...	...	
21	1.4	2.5	0.5	-	-	-	0.1	Nov.
22	0.2	4.0	7.2	6.3	9.3	...	...	
23	1.2	1.7	1.3	1.1	6.1	4.5	4.1	Sept.
24	16.6	16.4	24.5	20.4	26.4	...	...	
25	31.9	31.5	27.9	7.3	8.5	4.9	1.1	Oct.
26	244.5	181.0	208.0	180.0	212.3	212.3	260.2	Dec.
27	11.1	10.2	7.2	3.6	2.5	2.0	0.3	Oct.
28	10.3	4.2	4.0	3.6	4.2	2.8	3.5	Aug.
29	5.3	4.5	3.7	2.4	8.3	...	...	

APPENDIX III: (Continued)

B. IMPORTS

$ million	1953	1954	1955	1956	1957	
Asia (continued)						
Indonesia	2.1	3.5	10.1	30.2	27.0	1
Japan	29.7	40.8	80.8	83.7	80.5	2
Malaya/ Singapore	34.3	28.5	37.8	43.1	52.2	3
Sarawak	–	1.5	2.2	2.1	2.2	4
Sabah	...	...	...	1.4	1.0	5
America						
U.S.A.	9.6	0.2	0.2	–	–	6
Canada	1.1	1.7	3.2	5.8	5.4	7
Argentina	–	–	–	1.1	0.3	8
Brazil	–	–	–	–	–	9
Cuba	–	–	–	–	–	10
Uruguay	...	–	0.1	–	–	11
Africa						
Egypt	0.6	0.8	0.9	11.1	20.6	12
Sudan	0.1	0.1	0.1	0.3	0.7	13
S.Africa	0.5	1.0	1.0	0.9	1.4	14
Algeria	–	–	–	1.7	2.6	15
Morocco	7.2	11.1	19.0	19.8	9.2	16
Tunisia	0.2	0.1	0.1	0.3	0.6	17
Ghana	–	–	0.1[a]	0.1[a]	0.9[a]	18
Kenya	–	–	–	–	–	19
Uganda	–	–	–	–	–	20
Tanganyika	–	–	–	–	–	21
Australasia						
Australia	4.3	4.1	4.5	4.6	5.8	22
New Zealand	0.5	0.6	0.8	0.9	1.0	23

a. Includes trade with Taiwan. b. Covers trade with China, Hong significant partner. c. Domestic exports only. ... Not available.

Sources U.N. Yearbook of International Trade Statistics, 1961, Issues and Quarterly Issue January 1963; Economist Intelligence Kong; Trade Statistics of Individual Countries.

FROM CHINA

	1958	1959	1960	1961	1962	1962	1963	Jan.
								to:
1	41.8	61.2	56.9	...	...	...	...	
2	54.4	18.9	20.7	30.9	46.0	46.0	74.6	Dec.
3	63.9	51.1	57.6	56.4	65.0	...	...	
4	3.3	4.2	5.0	6.4	7.9	...	...	
5	1.7	1.5	1.9	2.1	2.5	...	...	
6	-	-	-	-	-	-	-	
7	5.6	5.2	5.6	3.2	4.3	4.0	4.6	Nov.
8	-	-	-	0.2	...	...	-	Oct.
9	-	0.1	-	0.1	0.4	...	...	
10	-	-	-	-	...	...	...	
11	-	-	-	-	-	...	...	
12	25.1	23.7	19.5	18.9	19.2	4.6	8.6	Mar.
13	1.5	2.6	2.2	4.3	3.8	1.5	1.1	Apr.
14	4.0	2.0	2.3	3.5	3.3	...	...	
15	2.4	2.0	...	...	...	...	...	
16	13.3	6.6	7.1	8.6	8.9	...	...	
17	0.5[a]	1.4[a]	0.9[a]	1.3[a]	0.6[a]	0.4[a]	0.7[a]	June
18	1.1	2.2	3.0	2.4	3.8	2.4	1.6	Aug.
19	0.1	0.1	0.1	-	0.1	0.1	0.3	Dec.
20	-	-	-	-	-	-	0.9	"
21	-	-	-	-	-	-	0.3	"
22	8.2	8.4	10.8	7.2	10.7	10.7	15.2	Dec.
23	1.2	...	...	...	...	...	...	

Kong, Mongolia and Taiwan.   Of these Hong Kong was the only
- Nil or negligible.

published 1963; U.N. Direction of International Trade   Annual
Unit, Quarterly Economic Reviews of China, N. Korea, Hong

APPENDIX IV: PRINCIPAL ITEMS IN SINO-SOVIET TRADE

$ million	1955	1956	1957	1958	1959	1960	1961	1962
A. SOVIET EXPORTS								
Machinery & Equipment	229.6	304.7	271.6	318.0	597.5	504.3	108.1	27.3
1. Metal cutting lathes	2.1	4.3	2.4	7.0	6.6	3.4	1.0	0.07
2. Power equipment	8.1	7.2	3.9	9.7	18.7	14.6	6.5	0.8
a. Steam boilers	0.5	1.1	1.7	0.2	6.4	1.8	1.1	–
b. Locomotives	–	–	–	3.6	0.9	0.5	–	–
c. Steam turbines	–	–	–	1.6	4.4	3.8	1.7	0.5
d. Hydro-turbines	–	–	–	–	–	2.2	–	–
e. Marine diesels	2.8	2.2	0.9	0.6	1.5	0.7	0.1	–
3. Electro-technical equipment	5.4	3.1	3.9	3.1	6.3	7.0	2.1	0.5
4. Oil drilling equipment	13.2	19.2	12.8	10.9	7.6	6.2	0.7	–
5. Equipment & materials for complete plants	141.5	217.0	209.0	166.2	399.8	373.8	78.9	8.8
6. Fixtures	3.4	4.1	6.7	9.9	7.5	...	0.9	0.8
a. Ball bearings	2.3	1.3	1.9	1.7	5.1	3.4	1.9	0.7
7. Tractors & farm machinery	10.5	9.1	2.5	19.8	8.5	9.1	1.8	1.6
a. Tractors	7.2	5.9	0.5	10.8	2.6	4.2	0.2	0.1
b. Agricultural machinery	1.5	2.0	0.5	7.1	4.0	3.0	0.3	0.02
8. Railway rolling stock	0.4	1.5	0.3	5.0	75.7	5.4	0.4	–
9. Road vehicles & garage equipment	22.6	16.0	5.2	61.7	34.3	44.9	6.6	10.1
a. Trucks	15.7	9.4	1.4	51.8	25.4	36.1	2.1	4.8
b. Automobiles	1.3	1.1	0.4	2.1	2.7	1.9	0.06	0.2

APPENDIX IV: (Continued)

$ million	1955	1956	1957	1958	1959	1960	1961	1962
A. SOVIET EXPORTS (continued)								
10. Crude petroleum	14.1	14.8	14.2	15.0	13.7	12.1	–	–
11. Petroleum products	...	71.1	76.2	77.4	104.0	101.0	120.7	80.5
a. Gasoline	...	35.1	31.4	26.0	51.8	42.6	53.0	30.4
b. Kerosene	11.7	10.8	16.3	11.9	13.2	13.4	17.8	16.3
c. Diesel fuel	9.8	16.1	16.2	22.4	18.7	24.0	28.2	13.0
d. Oils & greases	8.4	8.6	11.7	17.0	19.6	18.3	20.2	19.5
12. Rolled ferrous metal	53.7	43.7	21.4	36.8	29.4	37.1	18.5	16.7
13. Pipes & tubes	12.4	12.1	6.4	16.2	14.4	13.6	8.6	6.9
14. Non-ferrous metals & alloys	6.9	10.1	1.4	10.7	1.7	3.2	2.7	2.8
15. Rolled non-ferrous metals	4.7	6.7	5.6	4.0	3.5	5.4	2.5	2.0
16. Cultural & domestic household goods	4.7	5.0	6.0	7.2	5.2	4.0	3.0	9.8
a. Domestic machines & appliances	0.3	0.3	1.9	4.5	2.4	0.6	0.3	7.6
b. Moving pictures	2.1	2.7	2.0	1.1	1.3	1.0	0.5	0.3
Total Exports (including other items)	748.4	733.1	544.1	634.9	954.6	817.1	367.3	233.5

APPENDIX IV: (Continued)

$ million	1955	1956	1957	1958	1959	1960	1961	1962
B. SOVIET IMPORTS								
1. Ships	10.3	9.2	6.4	4.3	12.1	-	-	-
2. Metal ores & concentrates	62.2	75.5	89.9	74.0	73.3	61.2	48.3	35.3
3. Non-metallic minerals	5.9	10.2	11.1	11.9	10.1	5.3	4.1	3.2
4. Ferrous metals	26.3	27.3	6.7	19.2	7.6	12.4	8.7	6.6
a. Cast iron	26.2	21.0	4.7	9.8	6.9	11.8	7.5	6.6
5. Non-ferrous metals & alloys	56.2	50.4	51.7	48.9	54.9	48.9	34.2	25.9
a. Tin	47.9	32.4	45.5	39.3	41.7	34.8	22.4	17.5
6. Chemical products	6.5	16.6	9.6	12.2	7.4	10.4	5.0	4.0
7. Building materials	6.3	9.5	15.4	18.0	12.7	13.1	13.4	14.8
8. Textile raw materials	59.5	58.6	49.0	37.5	91.6	65.3	22.8	13.9
a. Cotton	-	-	-	-	52.3	...	8.0	5.9
b. Wool	23.6	21.4	23.9	21.2	21.9	19.4	10.4	7.9
c. Silk	21.5	23.5	21.3	16.3	17.3	12.0	4.4	0.02

APPENDIX IV: (Continued)

$ million	1955	1956	1957	1958	1959	1960	1961	1962
B. SOVIET IMPORTS (continued)								
9. Raw hides	3.5	9.1	7.9	5.4	3.4	1.3	0.6	0.5
10. Industrial fats & oils	4.7	7.4	7.4	8.6	9.0	4.6	1.6	2.8
a. Tung oil	4.3	7.0	6.9	7.9	8.9	4.4	1.5	2.8
11. Bristle, animal hair etc.	17.2	14.6	11.0	14.6	16.4	10.0	3.0	1.2
a. Bristle	13.2	10.1	5.0	7.7	11.5	6.4	1.4	0.4
12. Oilseeds & products for industrial use	98.5	99.7	79.8	61.9	79.0	43.1	1.3	–
a. Groundnuts	39.2	35.8	18.9	7.8	7.1	4.2	–	–
b. Soya beans	47.5	53.6	55.5	50.1	67.4	35.7	1.0	–
13. Tea	10.6	12.5	12.2	15.6	19.4	13.0	2.7	2.8
14. Meat, butter, fats & eggs	73.2	66.8	40.8	80.3	46.9	19.5	1.9	–
a. Meat & meat products	68.7	63.1	33.8	66.6	42.1	18.5	1.9	–
16. Rice	41.2	64.3	25.4	60.8	82.6	55.2	0.3	20.4
17. Vegetables & fruit	15.0	20.3	27.1	32.7	31.2	18.2	9.6	13.0
18. Vegetable oils, edible	29.6	25.7	13.2	21.1	21.0	9.3	–	–

APPENDIX IV: (Continued)

$ million	1955	1956	1957	1958	1959	1960	1961	1962
B. SOVIET IMPORTS (continued)								
19. Cloth	43.4	65.7	86.1	87.2	155.5	139.5	126.3	118.4
a. Cotton	0.4	1.2	2.1	3.8	50.1	35.5	16.4	24.0
b. Wool	20.2	35.5	50.0	42.8	49.8	34.8	57.9	45.2
c. Silk	20.9	23.4	26.7	30.9	41.1	32.3	41.8	38.1
20. Outer garments & under clothing	15.2	28.5	46.7	97.9	198.9	192.0	175.3	181.1
a. Heavy & light outerwear	2.1	5.2	13.6	40.3	85.0	88.1	89.2	93.4
b. Knitted outer & underwear	1.9	4.6	9.9	22.8	52.5	60.1	53.7	52.3
c. Table & bed linen & towels	8.4	12.8	13.8	17.1	35.4	25.6	12.9	12.7
d. Blankets	1.9	4.2	7.5	9.6	12.6	11.7	11.6	8.5
21. Leather footwear	...	3.7	7.1	34.2	36.7	41.5	14.1	14.6
Total Imports (including other items)	643.5	764.2	738.1	881.3	1,100.3	848.1	551.5	516.3

... Not available.   – Nil.

<u>Source</u>   Soviet Trade Statistics.

APPENDIX V: MAJOR EXTENSIONS OF ECONOMIC AID BY CHINA

Date & Country	Total $ mn (rounded)	Grants & Gifts	Loans Amount	Interest % p.a.	Notes
		millions of currency stated			
1953[a] November					
Mongolia	72	Yuan 280[b]		—	Cancellation of outstanding trade debts
N. Korea	72	Yuan 280[b]		—	Cancellation of outstanding trade debts
" "	205	Yuan 800[b]		*	Economic aid to be spread over four years – 1954–57.
1954[c]					
Albania	15	Roubles (old) 10	Roubles (old) 50	?	To be used during 1955–60.
1955 July					
N. Vietnam	205	Yuan 800[b]		*	To finance railway construction 1955–59.
1956 May					
Cambodia	22	Riels 800		?	To build factories during 1956–57. The first aid given to a non-communist country.
1956 August					
Mongolia	40	Roubles (old) 160		*	To finance trade in the four years 1956–59.

APPENDIX V: (Continued)

Date & Country	Total $ mn (rounded)	Grants & Gifts	Loans Amount	Interest % p.a.	Notes
		millions of currency stated			
1956 October Nepal	13	Rupees 60		*	Given one third in Indian currency, two-thirds in Chinese goods and services over three years.
1956 November Egypt	5	Swiss francs 20		*	Given to help Egypt after the Suez crisis. Trade debt moratorium.
Indonesia	15				
1956 December Hungary	8	Roubles (old) 30		*	Given to help Hungary after the 1956 uprising.
1957 May Hungary	50		Roubles (old) 200	2	Half made available in free currency, the remainder in Chinese goods. Repayment 1960–69.
1957 September Ceylon	16	Rupees 75		*	To finance over a five-year period rubber replanting, to build a textile

APPENDIX V. (Continued)

Date & Country	Total $ mn (rounded)	Grants & Gifts	Loans Amount	Interest % p.a.	Notes
		millions of currency stated			
1957 September Ceylon (continued)					mill, to obtain rolling stock etc. The agreement expired before all the grant had been used and was therefore (in May 1962) extended for a further five years – from 1.1.63. to 31.12.67.
1958 January Burma	4		Kyats 20	2.5	To build a cotton mill, which came into full three-shift operation in September 1959.
Yemen	16		Swiss francs 70	nil	To finance road-building, industrial re-construction and trade. Repayable over ten years. The Sanaa-Hodeida highway, begun in 1958, was completed in January 1962, but other projects did not get under way. It was therefore decided in 1962 that the remainder of the money should be employed in road maintenance and the building of a spinning and a weaving mill.

APPENDIX V: (Continued)

Date & Country	Total $ mn (rounded)	Grants & Gifts	Loans Amount	Interest % p.a.	Notes
		millions of currency stated			
1958 April Indonesia	11		Swiss francs 48	2.5	To buy rice and cotton piecegoods. Re-payable in ten years.
1958 September Ceylon	11		Rupees 50	2.5	For the supply of complete plant and goods over four years; repayable in Ceylonese goods 1961–70. As the loan has not been fully used, the Ceylon government in August 1962 requested that it be extended for a further three years to September 1965.
N. Korea	10		Roubles (old) 40	nil	To build a hydro-electric power station. Repayable 1968–77
N. Korea	43		Roubles (old) 170	1	To build a textile mill and two paper mills. Repayable by 1970.
1958 December Mongolia	25		Roubles (old) 100	2.5	To buy equipment for textile mills and power plants in 1959–61. Repayable in fifteen years.

APPENDIX V: (Continued)

Date & Country	Total $ mn (rounded)	Grants & Gifts millions of currency stated	Loans Amount millions of currency stated	Interest % p.a.	Notes
1959[d] January					
Albania	14		Roubles (old) 55	?	To finance trade 1961–65.
1959[d] February					
N. Vietnam	26	Yuan 100[b]		*	To finance industrial construction.
" "	75		Yuan 800[b]	1	To finance industrial construction.
Indonesia	30		$ 30	2.5	To buy equipment for textile mills; re-payable in fifteen years. Confirmed in 1961.
1960 March					
Nepal	21	Rupees 100		*	To build a paper mill and cement factory in 1960–62. At the end of 1963 it was decided to abandon these projects; Chinese experts went to Nepal to discuss alternative ventures.
1960 May					
Mongolia	50	Roubles (old) 200		–	Trade debt cancellation.

APPENDIX V: (Continued)

Date & Country	Total $ mn (rounded)	Grants & Gifts millions of currency stated	Loans Amount	Loans Interest % p.a.	Notes
1960 September Guinea	25		Roubles (old) 100	nil	To be used 1960–63 for projects agreed by both sides. Repayment 1970–79 either in Guinean francs or other currency acceptable to China.
1960 October N. Korea	105		Roubles (old) 420	?	To be used 1961–64 to finance building plants to make rubber tyres, radio communications equipment and a variety of consumer goods. China to supply technical experts, machines and plant.
1960 November Cuba	60		Roubles (old) 420	nil	To buy complete sets of equipment and to pay for technical aid, 1961–65.
Congo	3	$3			

APPENDIX V: (Continued)

Date & Country	Total $ mn (rounded)	Grants & Gifts	Loans Amount	Interest % p.a.	Notes
		millions of currency stated			
1961 January Cambodia	11	£4		*	To complete four factories begun with the help of aid given in 1956.
Burma	83		Kyats 400	nil	To buy complete plant and to pay for technical aid in 1961–67. Repayment to start in 1971 and be completed by 1980. Chinese experts surveyed sites and in 1963 agreed a list of projects with the Burmese government to be financed with this loan.
N. Vietnam [e]	158		Roubles (new) 141.75	?	To help with the five-year development plan announced in September 1960.
1961 May Albania	125		$125	?	To buy industrial equipment to build chemical, electrical and metallurgical plants.
1961 August Ghana	20		£7	nil	To buy over the next five years plant

APPENDIX V. (Continued)

Date & Country	Total $ mn (rounded)	Grants & Gifts	Loans Amount	Interest % p.a.	Notes
		millions of currency stated			
1961 August Ghana (continued)					and equipment, to pay for Chinese experts and technicians and the training of Ghanaians in China. Re-payable in ten equal instalments, 1971–81, in Ghanaian goods or a currency acceptable to China.
1961 September Mali	20		$20	?	Economic and technical agreement signed September 1961. Protocol to agreement signed 11.11.62. The money is to be used during 1962–67 and repaid during 1971–81.
Indonesia	20		£7	2	Protocol covering use of aid offered in 1959. To buy equipment, material and technical assistance in connection with six spinning mills and seven weaving plants. Repayable in five years after completion of the projects. The terms are slightly different from those pro–

APPENDIX V: (Continued)

Date & Country	Total $ mn (rounded)	Grants & Gifts	Loans Amount	Interest % p.a.	Notes
		millions of currency stated	millions of currency stated		
1961 September Indonesia (continued)					posed in 1959. The 1959 loan of $30 million was also confirmed (see above).
1961 November Nepal	10	£3.5		*	To cover the cost of technicians, materials and machinery needed for the Nepal stretch of the Kathmandu-Lhasa road. The Nepalese side of this project has hung fire and the road will be opened to traffic at earliest in 1967, two years later than the original Chinese plan.
1962 January Laos	?	?		*	Highway built to link Laos with Yunnan. Completed early 1963.
Ceylon					1957 and 1958 agreements extended (see above).
Yemen					1958 agreement extended.

APPENDIX V: (Continued)

Date & Country	Total $ mn (rounded)	Grants & Gifts millions of currency stated	Loans Amount	Interest % p.a.	Notes
1963 May Burma					Agreements on projects under 1961 aid (see above).
1963 June Syria	16		Swiss francs 70	nil	To be used to buy Chinese equipment. Repayable in ten annual instalments.
1963 September Somalia	20		£7.2	nil	Chinese teams of experts are searching the country for worthwhile projects.
"	3	£1			To cover budget deficit in place of former British grant.
1963 October Algeria	51		Francs (old) 25,000	nil	To be used to build a Saharan road system and to construct small industries. To be repaid 1970–89.

APPENDIX V: (Continued)

Date & Country	Total $ mn (rounded)	Grants & Gifts millions of currency stated	Loans Amount	Interest % p.a.	Notes
1963 May Cuba	?		?	nil	Long-term interest-free loan to the amount of China's surplus on trade with Cuba in 1962 and 1963.
1964 February Zanzibar	0.5		£185,000	?	At the time of writing it was not clear whether this is a gift or a loan or on what terms it was accepted. It is reported to be the forerunner of more.

* Indicates grant.

a. An unknown quantity of aid was given to Albania in 1953.   b. Converted at 0.975 yuan=1 (old) rouble, 4 roubles=$1.
c. An unknown quantity of aid was given to North Vietnam in this year.   d. Help was given to the Algerians in this year; it was variously reported as from $5 million to $10 million.   e. Later in the same year China is believed to have extended military aid and possibly to have agreed to the cancellation of further trade debts.

Principal Sources Hsinhua News Agency; Far Eastern Economic Review; Economist Intelligence Unit, Quarterly Economic Reviews of China, North Korea, Hong Kong; press reports from various countries.

SELECT BIBLIOGRAPHY

SELECT BIBLIOGRAPHY

a) Books

ALLEN, G.C. and DONNITHORNE, A. Western Enterprise in Far Eastern Economic Development. London:
George Allen & Unwin. 1954.

BARNETT, A.D. Communist Economic Strategy - The
Rise of Mainland China. Washington D.C.: National
Planning Association. 1959.

_____ Communist China in Perspective. New York:
Frederick A. Praeger. 1962.

CHENG, YU-KWEI. Foreign Trade and Industrial Development of China. An historical and integrated analysis
through 1948. University Press of Washington D.C.
1956.

ECKSTEIN, A. and others. The National Income of
Communist China. New York: The Free Press of
Glencoe Inc. 1961.

KIRBY, E.S. (ed). Contemporary China. Vol. III.
1958-59. Hong Kong University Press. Oxford
University Press. 1960.

LI, CHOH-MING. Economic Development of Communist
China - An appraisal of the first five years of indust-
rialization. Berkeley & Los Angeles: University of
California Press. 1959.

_____ The Statistical System of Communist China.
Berkeley & Loss Angeles: University of
California Press. 1962.

LI, FU-CHUN. Report on the First Five-Year Plan for
the Development of the National Economy of the
People's Republic of China for 1953-1957. Peking:
Foreign Language Press. 1955.

NOVE, A. and DONNELLY, D. Trade with Communist
Countries. London: Hutchinson & Co. Ltd. 1960.

ROSTOW, W.W. The Prospects for Communist China.
New York: pub. jointly by Massachusetts Institute of
Technology and John Wiley & Sons Inc. 1954.

SNOW, E. The Other Side of the River. London: Victor
Gollancz. 1963.

SZCZEPANIK, E.F. (ed). Symposium on Economic and
Social Problems of the Far East. Proceedings of a
meeting held in September 1961 as part of the Golden
jubilee Congress of the University of Hong Kong.
London: Oxford University Press. 1964.

WU, YUAN-LI, An Economic Survey of Communist China.
New York: Bookman Associates. 1956.

b) Official Publications

FOREIGN LANGUAGES PRESS: First Five-Year Plan for
the Development of the National Economy of the People's
Republic of China. 1953-1957. Peking 1956.

_____   Handbook on People's China. Peking 1957.

_____   Ten Great Years. Statistics of the Economic
and Cultural Achievements of the People's
Republic of China. Peking 1960.

UNITED NATIONS: Economic Survey of Asia and the Far
East (annual).

_____   Economic Bulletin for Asia & the Far East
(quarterly).

_____   World Economic Survey (annual).

_____   Statistical Yearbook.

_____   Yearbook of International Trade.

_____   Direction of International Trade (quarterly).

U.S. DEPARTMENT OF STATE: Mutual Defense Assistance
Control Act of 1951 - Annual Reports to Congress.

c) Other and Miscellaneous

CONGRESS FOR CULTURAL FREEDOM: The China
Quarterly Vols. 1-4, 1960-1963. Editorial and
business offices: Summit House, 1-2 Langham Place,
London, W.1. Published by the Congress for Cultural
Freedom, 104 Boulevard Haussmann, Paris 8[e].

ECONOMIST INTELLIGENCE UNIT: Quarterly Economic
Review of China, North Korea & Hong Kong 1952-1964.
Published by The Economist Intelligence Unit Limited,
Spencer House, 27 St. James's Place, London, S.W.1.